More profitable pricing

McGraw-Hill Finance Series

Consulting Editor
M. G. Wright

More profitable pricing

Arthur Marshall

McGRAW-HILL Book Company (UK) Limited

London · New York · St Louis · San Francisco · Auckland · Bogotá
Düsseldorf · Johannesburg · Lisbon · Lucerne · Madrid
Mexico · Montreal · New Delhi · Panama · Paris · San Juan
São Paulo · Singapore · Sydney · Tokyo · Toronto

Published by
McGraw-Hill Book Company (UK) Limited
MAIDENHEAD · BERKSHIRE · ENGLAND

British Library Cataloguing in Publication Data

Marshall, Arthur
    More profitable pricing.—(McGraw-Hill finance series).
    1. Price policy
    I. Title
    658.8'16   HF5416.5   78-41332

ISBN 0-07-084524-7

1 2 3 4 SB 81079

Printed and bound in Great Britain

Contents

1

Introduction

The theme of this work is *Pricing for profit improvement*. Its aim is to help you increase your profits by making the most advantageous use of available facilities.

Of all the business decisions a manufacturer has to make, the one that leaves him with the most abiding doubts is that of *pricing*.

This is not surprising when one considers that every season, or however frequently prices are fixed, it represents the moment of truth. It is the occasion on which the level of reward is set for all the planning, financing, designing, productive efficiency, skill, and quality that have gone into the product.

Yet a wrong guess at this time can cripple a business, no matter how otherwise efficient it might be.

Is it any wonder, then, that the manufacturer is beset by misgivings and hesitations?

The main reason for these doubts may well be that he is not one hundred per cent confident that his approach to pricing is the right one for him.

There are several approaches to pricing commonly used in industry, for example:

Supply and demand
Cost-plus
Following the market leader
Market and product analysis

The method most entrenched, and the one most likely to be used, is the cost-plus approach.

It will be seen from the following pages that the 'traditional' cost-plus methods of pricing are both questionable and illogical. At the best they may suffice in a sellers' market, where *costs* plus *profit* equals *price*, and where demand exceeds supply. In such conditions buyers can be found at any price that is not outrageously high, or high enough to cause the would-be buyer to look for an alternative, or forgo his want altogether.

But the traditional methods can be dangerously misleading in the changed circumstances of a buyers' market, where supply exceeds demand and the seller must get what price he can. From this price he must deduct his costs, and what remains (if anything) is his profit. Rigid adherence to the traditional cost-plus formulae in a buyers' market can result in getting orders that are uneconomic, and missing orders that would have been desirable.

The strange thing is that many manufacturers seem satisfied with such methods. Yet a major reason for differences between the profit results of otherwise similar companies can be traced to their pricing methods and policy.

To test this statement, during the course of a number of seminars some 40 teams, each of 3 executives, were subjected to the management exercise described in Appendix 1. This test was based on the same costs, production, and market information, yet widely divergent profit results were obtained.

Pricing is not, of course, the only consideration that may make a product attractive to a buyer.

Product attractions can be grouped broadly into five categories:

Design (shape, style, etc.)
Materials (fabrics, pattern, colour, etc.)
Quality (specification, skill, care, etc., put into product)
Availability (ex-stock or custom built)
Price

The order of precedence will depend very much on the circumstances at the time of purchase.

Does the buyer want it immediately? If so, *availability* may be more important than price.

Does it have to match something else? In this case, *design*, *materials*, and/or *quality* may assume greater importance.

Has the buyer limited cash with which to purchase the article? If so, *price* may be the dominant factor.

Where price is not the dominant consideration, it may well be that premium prices could be obtained. But rigid formula prices make no provision for these other ways in which products attract buyers.

In general, businessmen would rather compete on non-price factors than they would on price. It is much more difficult to make price comparisons for style goods than it is for staple goods. Also there is a belief that goodwill derived from the non-price factors is more enduring than that based on price appeal alone.

But in the last analysis, when one is selling substantially the same product, or offering the same service as someone else, then price is most likely to decide who gets the business and who does not.

In circumstances where the right prices are predominantly responsible for the generation of business, then the following holds true.

Pricing decides
  What products will be sold
  The volume of sales
  The profit from sales

In more detailed terms, then,

Pricing specifies
 The equipment to be operated
 Inventory commitments
 Expectable cash flow
 What sales effort is required
 Which markets can be sold to
 Probable returns on capital

Pricing, therefore, is no small responsibility. It should not be lightly delegated as some irksome necessity, unless management realizes that, at the same time, it is delegating to the same people full responsibility for the effective employment of the company's capital and resources.

Traditional pricing methods

You may ask why, if the traditional methods of selling price build-up are so dangerously misleading, they are in such common use.

This is partly due to a much too prevalent assumption that selling prices are *cost based*. Such a belief has survived in those industries where for 25 years the problem has been to increase productivity to satisfy expanding markets. Yet cost is only one of several factors that determine a selling price. In certain market conditions, demand may be a most potent factor, while in other conditions the extent of competition may be critical.

The survival of the traditional cost-plus methods is also partly due to management's attitude towards pricing. Management tends to look for short cuts, considering time and involvement in paperwork as a sign of inefficiency and something to be minimized.

Certainly, the cost-plus methods are administratively easy to apply, and superficially appear to ensure a certain overall profit margin. They avoid the need to treat each product on its merits and, once the mark-ups have been agreed (perhaps on an annual or seasonal basis), no further decision is necessary. The complete process can be delegated.

The average executive is attracted by formulae and guidelines that offer the promise of a speedy solution to his problems. This is very understandable considering the number of matters competing daily for his attention. But management should realize that the cost-plus approach does not lead to the optimization of profits.

Many managing directors do not ordinarily concern themselves with pricing details; some are even not particularly aware of how their products are priced. Yet pricing a product is one of the most critical decisions management is called upon to make.

There are many ways cash can flow out of a business—but only one way it flows in—through prices.

Let us consider now what the 'traditional' methods have to offer.

Envisage asking your accountant, your cost clerk, your estimator, or whoever builds up your selling prices, for a price for a certain product. Imagine he came back to you with a schedule of 10 prices with a range of 30 per cent between the highest and the lowest (see Fig. 2.1). What would you think?

Yet this is perfectly feasible, using the traditional methods of price build-up, as Fig. 2.9 page 10, shows.

How this comes to be is explained in the following pages.

Method	Price
1.1	£13.05
2.1	13.05
3.1	12.00
4.1	12.42
5.1	10.68
1.2	13.92
2.2	13.92
3.2	12.80
4.2	13.24
5.2	11.40
Difference: lowest/highest	30%

Fig. 2.1. Schedule of prices for Product A

FULL COSTING

The traditional method of pricing, shown in Fig. 2.2, is to take the materials and labour content of a product, add to this an allocation of overhead expenses to arrive at a 'full' cost, and then apply a mark-up to convert the 'full' cost into a selling price.

Materials content	××
Labour content	××
Overheads	××
'Full' cost	×××
+ Margin (mark-up)	××
SELLING PRICE	×××

Fig. 2.2. Traditional cost-plus selling price build-up

The materials and labour content may be close to fact, but the allocation of overheads is an arbitrary decision based on at least two estimates:

1. The level of overhead expenses covering the future period in which the product will be made.
2. The level of activity over which the overheads should be recovered.

Because it is planned that the budgeted overheads will be fully absorbed by the budgeted production, this traditional method of cost build-up is often known as *absorption costing*.

There are several different formulae for absorbing overheads into unit product costs, each one of which is perfectly capable of justification, but all of which can give different answers. These formulae include, for example:

1. Percentage on direct labour value
2. Rate per direct labour hour
3. Rate per unit of product
4. Percentage on prime cost
5. Rate per machine hour

Formula number 1 can be further subdivided into those using *standard direct*

5

labour value, and those using *actual direct labour value*. Similarly, formula number 2 can be subdivided into those using *standard direct labour hours*, and those using *actual direct labour hours*.

Using the basic data from Fig. 2.3, let us see the relative results of using the various traditional formulae.

Materials	£60 000 p.a.
Labour	£40 000 p.a.
Overheads	£84 000 p.a.
Direct labour hours	50 000 hours
Machine hours	40 000 hours
Units p.a.	20 000 units
Direct labour rate per hour	80p

Fig. 2.3. Data on costs and production

Formula 1

$$\frac{\text{Overheads}}{\text{Labour}} \quad \frac{£84\,000}{£40\,000} \times 100 = 210\%$$

Application

	Product A	Product B
Material	£3.00	£3.00
Labour	2.40	1.20
Overheads (210%)	5.04	2.52
'FULL' COST	£10.44	£6.72

Fig. 2.4. Formula 1: Percentage on direct labour value

The underlying assumption of Formula 1, shown in Fig. 2.4, is that the incidence of overhead expenditure is directly related to labour cost. If labour received a 15 per cent wage increase, the overheads recovered would also increase by 15 per cent. But many of the overhead expenses are fixed (rents, depreciation, etc.) and would probably not vary in the same time scale. In such circumstances, the over-recovery of overheads may force the price so high that it becomes non-competitive and orders are lost.

As long as the labour cost per hour stays the same as was originally envisaged—i.e., 80p per hour—the result of Formula 2 in Fig. 2.5 will appear the same as Formula 1.

However, as soon as the wage rate per hour alters, the two formulae will show different results, as Formula 1 will then be applying a percentage to a changing direct labour value.

6

Formula 2

$$\frac{\text{Overheads}}{\text{Direct labour hours}} \quad \frac{£84\ 000}{50\ 000} = £1.68 \text{ per hour}$$

Application

	Product A	Product B
Materials	3.00	3.00
Labour (A) 3 hrs	2.40	
(B) 1½ hrs		1.20
Overheads		
(A) 3 × £1.68	5.04	
(B) 1½ × £1.68		2.52
'FULL' COST	£10.44	£6.72

Fig. 2.5. Formula 2: Rate per direct labour hour

Formula 3

$$\frac{\text{Overheads}}{\text{Units}} \quad \frac{£84\ 000}{20\ 000} = £4.20 \text{ per unit}$$

Application

	Product A	Product B
Material and labour	£5.40	£4.20
Overheads (per unit)	4.20	4.20
'FULL' COST	£9.60	£8.40

Fig. 2.6. Formula 3: Unit cost method

While the simplicity of Formula 3, shown in Fig. 2.6, may appeal strongly, it is only really usable where the product made is identical to all the other products made. Even then, if, at the time of calculating the overhead recovery per unit, the market seems poor and a gloomy view is taken of the number of units saleable, the overheads per unit will be high, and the resultant selling price will also be high.

On the other hand, if the economy is very buoyant, and the view is that many units can be sold, then the overheads will be recoverable over a larger number of units. The total cost, and consequently the selling price, will be lower.

The effect of using Formula 3, therefore, is that when sales are difficult the selling price is high, and when everything can be sold the selling price is low. "The arithmetic is faultless, but the pricing strategy is crazy."

Consider what could happen using Formula 3 when pricing is in the hands of the 'traditionalists'. The recommended actions can sometimes be most unbusinesslike.

Example

(a) Materials and labour cost	£5.40 per unit	
(b) Overheads	£84 000 p.a.	

	Good times	Bad times
(c) Output (units)	20 000 p.a.	12 000 p.a.
(d) Materials and labour costs per unit	£5.40	£5.40
(e) Overheads (b ÷ c)	4.20	7.00
TOTAL COST	9.60	12.40
25% mark-up	2.40	3.10
SELLING PRICE	£12.00	£15.50

Let us assume £12.00 is below competition and so sales increase rapidly to, say, 30 000 units a year. The selling price build-up would be:

Materials and labour cost	£5.40
Overheads £84 000 ÷ 30 000 =	2.80
TOTAL COST	8.20
25% mark-up	2.05
SELLING PRICE	£10.25

When the accountant gives this new selling price to management, he is, in effect, telling them to reduce prices despite the rapid increase in sales.

Formula 4

$$\frac{\text{Overheads £84 000} \times 100}{\text{Materials £60 000} + \text{Labour £40 000}} = 84\%$$

Application

	Product A	Product B
Prime cost (Materials and labour)	£5.40	£4.20
Overheads 84%	4.53	3.53
'FULL' COST	£9.93	£7.73

Fig. 2.7. **Formula 4: Percentage on prime cost**

The underlying implication of Formula 4 (see Fig. 2.7) is that the incidence of overhead expenses is in some way directly related to the value of labour and materials.

8

This theory is patently nonsense. If one used materials which were twice as expensive, what possible influence would this have on the majority of overhead expenses—management salaries, rents, rates, depreciation, for example? The only possible expense that might be affected would be interest on the use of money. A simple test comparing interest with the total of overhead expenses would soon put this into perspective.

The real danger in applying Formula 4 is that goods made from expensive materials may be over-priced, with the consequent danger of losing the market, and that goods made from inexpensive materials may be under-priced. The latter situation could result in a bumper order book, a factory filled with under-priced goods, and consequent failure to recover fully overhead expenses and profits. If, through greater efficiency in the buying or use of materials, the materials cost is reduced by £1.00, then the full cost will be reduced by £1.84. If a mark-up of 25 per cent is normally applied to 'full' cost to arrive at a selling price (see page 10), then the ultimate reduction in the selling price will be £1.84 + 25% = £2.30. A poor reward for saving £1.00 by more efficient use of materials.

Formula 5

$$\frac{\text{Overheads}}{\text{Machine hours}} \quad \frac{£84\ 000}{40\ 000} = £2.10 \text{ per m/c hour}$$

Application

	Product A	Product B
Material and labour	£5.40	£4.20
Overheads (£2.10 per m/c hour)		
A. 1½ hours × £2.10	3.15	
B. 2¼ hours × £2.10		4.70
'FULL' COST	£8.55	£8.90

Fig. 2.8. Formula 5: Machine-hour rate

Formula 5 (see Fig. 2.8): by seeking to absorb overhead expenses into unit product costs on the basis of each product's use of machine hours, is, in effect, assuming a direct relativity between the incidence of overhead expenses and the availability of machine hours. But such expenses as management salaries, rents, rates, heating and lighting, etc., can rise even though the quantity of available machine hours be the same or even reduced.

A practical difficulty in the use of the machine-hour basis of overhead absorption in a production shop with a mixture of different machines is to find an equitable basis for relating the quality of one machine hour to another where there are

1. Different levels of investment in the various machines
2. Different space requirements
3. Different productive capacities

Many of these formulae for allocating overheads to the product have an inherent weakness. They are based on budgeted levels of expense and volumes of production.

As stated earlier, in good times, when an optimistic view is taken of business, the budgeted overheads are divided by a large number of units. Consequently the overheads per product are low, and hence the 'full' cost and the resulting selling prices are also low.

In hard times, when a pessimistic view of business is taken, the budgeted overheads are divided by a lower number of units. Hence the cost and the resulting selling price are higher.

The result is that in good times, when orders are easy to get, the formula prices are lower; in hard times, when orders are difficult, prices are higher.

So far, we have considered the use of the various formulae in arriving at a 'full' unit cost. Now we have to add the second element of the cost-plus: the 'plus' bit, in other words, the profit.

Even at this stage, manufacturers may mean different things when they speak of a 'margin' or 'mark-up'. When they speak of a 25 per cent margin, they may mean 25 per cent on 'full' cost, or 25 per cent on selling price. And there is a substantial difference between the two.

	25% on cost £	25% on selling price £
Cost	8.55	8.55
Plus	2.14	2.85
SELLING PRICE	10.69	11.40

Is it any wonder, then, that firms that otherwise appear very similar produce such different prices and profit results?

Applying the two versions of margin to the various methods of calculating 'full' cost illustrated earlier, the formula selling prices shown in Fig. 2.9 are obtained.

	Product A	Product B
1. 25% on 'full' cost:		
Formula 1	£13.05	£8.40
2	13.05	8.40
3	12.00	10.50
4	12.41	9.66
5	10.69	11.13
2. 25% on selling price (i.e., $33\frac{1}{3}$% on 'full' cost):		
Formula 1	£13.92	£8.96
2	13.92	8.96
3	12.80	11.20
4	13.24	10.31
5	11.40	11.87
Difference: highest/lowest	30%	41%

Fig. 2.9. Formula selling prices

Of course, the accountant has to choose some method to calculate cost price, and will give a single figure, with its illusion of accuracy. An equally 'accurate' cost could be 30 to 40 per cent different.

Price competition comes more from costing/pricing methods than from any inherent qualities of the products.

Defects of traditional cost-plus methods

1. No cause-and-effect relationship exists between overheads to be distributed and basis of apportionment.
2. No allowance is made for any differences in extent to which key facilities may be used.
3. They provide no knowledge of the price floor, and therefore cannot meet competition intelligently.
4. They ignore competitive prices and customer demand.
5. They over-price products in periods of unfavourable economic conditions.
6. They under-price products in periods of better economic conditions.
7. They give the illusion of being absolutely accurate, while in fact different methods may produce 'accurate' costs up to 30 per cent different.

There is a general tendency for firms which use the cost-plus approach to treat the price so calculated as a maximum one, and to move prices downwards if they are under market pressure.

The response to the market is only in one direction.

Obviously, there is more to selling prices than simply marking up so-called 'costs'.

Towards a new method of pricing

To overcome the defects mentioned above, any proposed method of pricing must satisfy certain requirements.

1. It must not pretend that there is a cause-and-effect relationship between overheads to be distributed and the basis of apportionment.
2. It must recognize that the availability of key facilities sets practical limits to the productive capacity.
3. It must recognize differences in the extent to which the product being priced occupies those key facilities.
4. It must provide a knowledge of the price floor, so that competition can be met intelligently.
5. It must recognize the existence of competition, and that this may mean more flexible pricing. Yet it must provide a means of control so that, if more flexible pricing is necessary, the attainment of profit goals can still be monitored.

Later chapters outline a method which recognizes the realities of the existing situation, and any changes that may happen as a result of the acceptance of an order for the company's products.

The proposed method acknowledges that certain productive facilities exist (plant, machinery, etc.), and that the maintenance of these facilities will incur costs which will not vary significantly whether an order is got or not. To that extent, these costs are *fixed costs*.

The proposed method also recognizes that certain costs will be incurred because an order is obtained. These costs are for materials, direct labour, packaging, distribution, commission and discount, etc. In the main, these costs are avoidable if the order is not booked. They are called *variable costs*.

Any excess of selling price over variable costs makes a contribution towards the payment of the fixed costs of the existing facilities.

When the aggregate of all the contributions from all the products sold exceeds the fixed costs of the business, that excess is *profit*. Therefore:

Selling price − Variable costs = Contribution

Our more rational pricing method is based on restructuring this formula so that:

Variable costs + Contribution = Selling price

But, first of all, we ought to consider the nature of selling prices, and how they are influenced by various factors.

3

What is a selling price?

A definition of selling price might read:

'A selling price is the amount of money which a willing seller can obtain from a willing buyer in exchange for the product on offer.'

It could be even more simple:

'The selling price is the amount that someone is prepared to pay for an article.'

Even more succinctly,

'A selling price is what you can get for something.'

But for our purposes, such an over-simplified definition is somewhat lacking, in so far as it could also embrace the activities of pressure salesmen and con-men. A more acceptable definition could be:

'The right price is the one that enables you to sell your goods, yielding an acceptable margin of profit, at the same time giving the customer the feeling of getting value for money and thereby retaining his goodwill.'

There is both art and science in deciding the right price, but the basic principle must be to equate profitability with goodwill and repeat business.

A selling price, therefore, is the result of a number of considerations by both parties to the transaction.

1. What the buyer is willing to pay for the article, bearing in mind,
   (a) How readily available an alternative is.
   (b) How the alternative compares in
       (i) quality and reliability
       (ii) design
       (iii) price.
2. What the seller is willing to sell it for, bearing in mind,
   (a) his costs of manufacture
   (b) the possibility of changing his production facilities over to more profitable products
   (c) the existence and extent of competition
   (d) the need for avoiding the build-up of slow-moving inventories.

Some of these factors are now considered in more detail.

To what extent do costs determine a selling price?

A seller's costs are specific to his own organization and method of working. His competitors' costs will almost certainly be different. It follows, therefore, that, if a seller has five competitors, there could be six different levels of cost for a similar product.

Can a buyer be expected to agree different prices from various sellers because their costs are different? He really is not greatly concerned what a seller's costs are, as long as he has a reliable alternative source of supply at competitive prices.

A seller's costs are peculiar to himself.

Prices, on the other hand, represent the community of competition in the seller's markets.

For a seller to arrive at a selling price by arbitrarily marking up some rigid cost formula is tantamount to denying the existence of this competition and market demand.

Let us consider the relationship of costs to selling prices in two situations: a sellers' market (Fig. 3.1), and a buyers' market (Fig. 3.2).

Manufacturer	Qty to sell	Cost price	Selling price	Value
		£	£	£
A	400	7.2	9.0	3 600
B	500	6.0	7.5	3 750
C	200	5.6	7.0	1 400
D	300	6.4	8.0	2 400
Total availability	1 400	or	£7.76	£11 150
Market, say	1 800			

Fig. 3.1. Costs and selling prices in a sellers' market

Figure 3.1 envisages a situation in which demand is for 1800 articles and supply is only 1400. Had the market information of the manufacturers been perfect, all could have got £9.00 per article.

Manufacturer	Qty to sell	Cost price	Selling price	Orders
A	400	7.2	9.0	
B	500	6.0	7.5	500
C	200	5.6	7.0	200
D	300	6.4	8.0	
Availability	1 400			
Market, say	1 000			

Fig. 3.2. Costs and selling prices in a buyers' market

In the situation set out in Fig. 3.2, however, manufacturers B and C would probably get their price but, if the buyers appreciate the market situation, A and D are unlikely to get their formula selling price. Together they have available 700 units, while the remainder of the market unsatisfied by B and C is only 300 units. The competition between them is likely to be quite intense, and they must choose whether to stick to the formula selling price—thereby missing orders—or depart from their formula price and minimize their losses. Any failure to obtain the orders on which the original costs were based would inevitably mean that the fixed costs would have to be recovered over fewer units, which in turn would push up costs.

Looking at these two examples, of what use have costs been in arriving at the selling prices?

In Fig. 3.1, the sellers' market, better prices could have been obtained than those asked for as a result of formula pricing, and in Fig. 3.2, the buyers' market, formula selling price build-ups can be quickly abandoned when capacity exceeds demand.

It is true that, in the long run, a man needs an income greater than his costs to stay in business. But in a very competitive world his aim should be to make sure his costs are less than the going market price, rather than the other way around.

Although costs should not be the *sole* determining factor in arriving at a selling price, they do have an important role to play. As will be seen later, there is still a need for objective, traceable cost information to measure how much an order will contribute to profits if a 'going' market price is met. Information on costs is needed to help decide whether to accept a market price or withdraw the product on offer.

To what extent does competition determine price?

The extent to which competition influences selling prices can depend very much on how easy or difficult it is for a competitor to match one's products.

Generally, competition is much keener in the simpler, more easily made, staple goods, and much less keen in the making of 'specials'.

If the productive capacity of an industry is greater than demand, and competitors have expensive machines needing volume to cover their costs, then competition will be severe and prices keen.

To what extent does demand determine price?

The economists would have us believe that price is determined by the balance between supply and demand. If supply exceeds demand, prices fall until the two are in balance; if demand exceeds supply, prices rise.

The attempt to use this classical theory of demand as a basis for pricing decisions necessitates a number of assumptions which have only partial validity in day-to-day business practice.

These assumptions are:

1. Buyers and sellers have complete knowledge about the state of the market.
2. Demand and supply are uniformly distributed.
3. Buying and selling are rational processes, with price and quantifiable performance the only relevant factors.
4. The market is in equilibrium.

Buyers and sellers, more often than not, rely on their feeling about the state of the market, rather than on certain knowledge.

Buying is often based on last year's business, in the hope that the previous trend of demand will be a reliable guide. When that demand fails to materialize, off-take from the manufacturers is considerably retarded and the interrelationship between supply and demand is painfully readjusted.

Real markets are always in a state of disequilibrium, sometimes even in a state of instability.

Supply is not uniform, nor is demand. Convenience of purchase will often justify a price margin. Although easy and cheap transport tended to reduce such inequalities, it did not eliminate them. However, as transport becomes more expensive and adds to the cost of purchase, availability could again justify a price margin.

Supply and demand pricing applies only in special circumstances—more so in basic commodities, e.g., coffee, sugar, tin, copper, etc., than in industrial goods.

What determines a selling price?

The truth is that a selling price is greatly influenced by a number of factors, the relative importance of which may change from time to time:

1. Costs
2. Competition
3. Market demand and conditions
4. Financial liquidity ⎱ Is the seller in desperate need of turning
5. Inventory pressures ⎰ his stocks into cash?
6. Available productive capacity ⎱ To what extent does the seller need to
7. Investment in production lines ⎰ keep hungry machines busy?

All these factors can influence prices, and woe betide anyone who adheres rigidly to a pricing formula which ignores the existence of these influences.

4

The art and science of pricing

Pricing requires a combination of calculation and judgement.

In so far as a *science* is ... 'the pursuit of systematic and formulated knowledge', the science in pricing is involved in the organization of internally generated information on costs, profit sources, etc.

This 'scientific' aspect embraces:

1. Cost calculation: the recognition and measurement of variable costs and fixed costs, and the effect of volume changes thereon.
2. Measurement of contributions.
3. Profit planning: planning the volumes, product mix, and the optimum use of facilities.
4. Cost control: analysing variations from expected costs and arranging for them to be eliminated or minimized.

On the other hand, in as much as *art* is ... 'the exercise of skill and imagination', the pricer must be strategically artful in the way he handles this information and relates it to the external, unpredictable, uncertain events of the market place.

The strategic factors to be considered are:

1. The reaction from competitors.
2. The effect of the price level in the market.
3. The effect on the other phases of the seller's business, e.g., the displacement of more profitable work if the price attracts an order that is large and competes for the use of the same facilities.

Pricing involves the systematic collection of market information and statistics, and the skilful interpretation and use of this knowledge.

It needs both fact-gatherers and interpreters. It is neither the sole preserve of the cost accountant nor the monopoly of the sales manager. But it is an area where success demands the closest liaison between both functions if optimum profits are to be attained.

The pricer must know his product, the segment of the market he is aiming for, his customers, and the likely response of demand to any change in price.

Together the 'artist' and the 'scientist' must study the price-sensitivity of demand for their product, realizing that such price-sensitivity can be influenced by several factors, in the consideration of which both have their part to play.

These factors are:

1. The importance of the product to the customer.
2. The saturation level of need for the product.
3. The income bracket of the present consumer of the product.
4. The existence of substitutes for the product.
5. Whether the demand for the product is a *derived demand*, i.e., is based on demand for another product.

The pricing team must weigh each of these factors in relation to their own product.

Importance of product to customer
Certain products may be very important, in as much as they represent the necessities of life—e.g., basic foodstuffs, light, heat, accommodation, petrol for commuting, or bus and train fares, cigarettes (to some people), haircuts, etc.

While it may be true that people will pay as little as they have to for their needs, and may be rather more extravagant on the things they want, the demand for necessities may not be very price sensitive. In the last resort, the customer merely digs deeper into his pocket, forgoing or postponing the less important purchases.

Market saturation
If everyone is eating all the bread or drinking all the milk they can, it is unlikely that a price reduction will stimulate further demand. On the other hand, the demand for some products is far from filled. For example, price reductions for smaller automobiles could encourage the growth of two- or even three-car families.

Customers' income profile
In the case of the very rich, moderate changes in the price of their Rolls-Royce cars may not significantly alter demand. On the other hand, the demand for an inexpensive family car may be highly price-sensitive. A reduction in price may open up a new market by bringing the product within the range of a new income group, previously excluded by price.

Substitution
There comes a time when technological developments create substitutes, but customers, either through inertia or for lack of a market leader, may be slow to change.

Continual increases in the price of the original product may spur the customer to accept the change. If you are the manufacturer of the original product, the possibility of such a substitution and the avoidance of its encouragement may be a heavy consideration indeed.

Derived demand

If your product is a component part of a larger product then the demand for your product is most likely related to the demand for the larger product.

If your product is only a small part of the ultimate product, demand may not be particularly price-sensitive. The importance of the price of your component may depend on its influence on final costs. To what extent is the high-class shoe manufacturer going to worry about the 20 pence per thousand increase in the cost of shoe laces? How far is the suit manufacturer going to resist a small increase in the price per thousand of buttons?

Methodical consideration of factors such as the foregoing helps a supplier to find his place in the market. But as well as considering the price-sensitivity of demand, there are other factors of which the pricer should be aware before taking his decisions.

Product life-cycle

The life-cycle of a product in the market goes through four phases:

Innovation
Development
Maturity
Decline

The price it can command is often highest in the early phases, and a price rise in the decline phase may only hasten its decline. It is part of the art of the pricer to be aware at which stage each of his products has arrived.

Market pattern

The pricer must attempt to assess any likely changes in the market pattern.
These changes may arise as a result of any of the following:

Price cutting
Product innovation
Product substitution
Product obsolescence
Government legislation
Changes in taste or fashion
Seasonal factors
Import quotas
Trade recessions
Strikes and disputes

He must therefore be a well-informed person, ever alert to what may affect his business. He must be flexible enough to change course if some unforeseen circumstance jeopardizes his original plans.

Competition

He must know enough about his competitors to be able to predict their reactions. He must be able to weigh their performance in the following fields:

Pricing strategy
Sales force strength
Advertising effectiveness
Product advantages
Parts reputation
Distribution facilities

Prices and profits

Pricing is based on an assessment of:

Costs
Demands
Competition

What the pricer needs to know about these is considered in the next chapter.

But getting the best prices one can does not necessarily, by itself, ensure profitability.

Profits come from balancing

Prices
Costs
Volumes
Product mix

These are discussed in later chapters.

Pricing decisions which integrate the company's costs and capacities with market strategy, business conditions, product variables, channels of distribution, and financial characteristics will determine the success or failure of a business.

Such integration, or coordination, is management's job and should not be delegated, by default, to some formula-bound cost clerk.

1. He may hang on to his price ranges and reduce quality to permit this.
2. He may shift price ranges as customers' income changes.
3. He may trade up in time of rising prices and incomes.

It is advisable to know into which categories your customers fall. If you have a mixture of all three, you must be prepared to drop some of them and seek others.

This leads straight into the question of whether you should seek a market for what you make well, or make what you can readily sell to your existing customers. Beware of the latter: it can result in an uneconomic hotchpotch of many qualities, volumes, and styles.

Elasticity of demand

The pricer needs to appreciate the fluctuations in demand that can result from price changes, or what is commonly known as the *elasticity of demand.*

Demand is considered to be *elastic* where a reduction in price results in a compensating or greater increase in volume. In such circumstances, one can stimulate unit sales by reducing prices.

Demand is considered to be relatively *inelastic* if a reduction in price does not result in a corresponding increase in volume. In such circumstances, a price reduction only results in reduced profits.

This is not to say that when demand is inelastic prices can be pushed up and up. There comes a point where the would-be buyer is forced to look for substitutes or just does without.

Figure 5.4 gives an example of how the elasticity of demand affects the most profitable price and volume of production for a product.

Units	×	Price	=	Turnover	−	Variable expenses	=	Contribution	−	Fixed expenses	=	Profit
		£		£		£		£		£		£
10		30		300		85		215		150		65
20		22		440		170		270		150		120
30		17.5		525		255		270		150		120
40		13.75		570		340		230		150		80
50		11.75		587		425		162		150		12

Fig. 5.4. Profitability and different price/volume combinations

Information about demand elasticity can be obtained by:

Estimation
Regression analysis, or tests in trial market segments
Customer interviews.

Figure 5.5 represents graphically the example from Fig. 5.4. The most profitable price/volume combination is where the sales turnover curve is most greatly in excess of the total cost curve

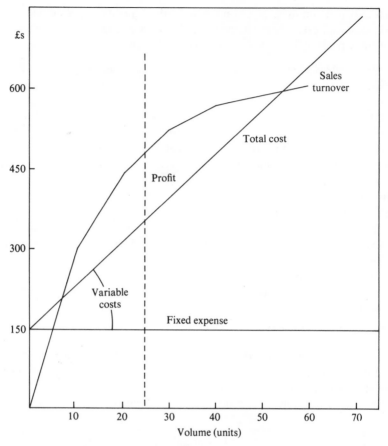

Fig. 5.5. Graph of possible price/volume combinations

Competition

A competitor's response to a pricing situation is dictated to some extent by his *costs structure*. In this context, costs structure is the proportion of fixed costs present in the total cost—i.e., the relationship between a company's fixed and variable costs.

Generally, where the demand for a product is elastic, a high fixed cost company is better placed to make higher profits (as a result of lower prices, lower unit profit margins, and higher volumes) than is a low fixed cost company.

But where the demand is inelastic, a low fixed cost company is better placed to make higher profits (out of price increases and volume reductions) than is a high fixed cost company.

Consider, for example, two companies, A and B, both initially making the same quantity, selling at the same price, and making the same profit. See how their fortunes change in three different situations. Company A has low fixed costs, and company B high fixed costs.

Situation 1

	Company A	Company B
Annual fixed cost	200 000	700 000
Annual variable cost	700 000	200 000
TOTAL COST	900 000	900 000
Profit	100 000	100 000
Annual sales turnover	£1 000 000	£1 000 000
Unit volume	100 000 units	100 000 units
Normal selling price per unit	£10	£10
Variable cost per unit	£7	£2
Unit contribution	£3	£8
Annual contribution	£300 000	£800 000
less fixed expenses	200 000	700 000
PROFIT	£100 000	£100 000

Now consider Situation 2, where the selling price has been dropped 15 per cent, (i.e., to £8.50) and the volume increased 30 per cent to 130 000 units—an 'elastic' situation.

Situation 2

	Company A	Company B
Price	£8.50	£8.50
Volume	130 000 units	130 000 units
New sales turnover	£1 105 000	£1 105 000
Variable cost per unit	£7	£2
New annual variable cost	910 000	260 000
New annual contribution	195 000	845 000
less fixed expenses	200 000	700 000
PROFIT (LOSS)	£(5 000)	£145 000

Now consider a third situation, where the selling price has been increased by 5 per cent (i.e., to £10.50) and this has resulted in a drop in volume to 90 000 units.

Situation 3

	Company A	Company B
Price	£10.50	£10.50
Volume	90 000 units	90 000 units
New sales turnover	£945 000	£945 000
Variable cost per unit	£7	£2
New annual variable cost	630 000	180 000
New annual contribution	315 000	765 000
less fixed costs	200 000	700 000
PROFIT	£115 000	£65 000

It is apparent from the above examples that a high fixed cost company needs *volume*, whereas a low fixed cost company is more dependent on *price*.

In which category are your competitors?

Information sources

If, as was suggested earlier, a selling price is what you can get, then in order to price effectively it is necessary to know what competitors are charging for their products. This can be relatively straightforward if the product is an advertised one, although even then there can be some uncertainty about what discounts are being granted to individual wholesalers and retailers.

Where product prices are not advertised, it is much more difficult.

For consumer goods, this information can be gained by systematic sampling of what a representative selection of stores are charging for similar products of comparable quality.

For goods made for industrial use, and indeed to supplement the above information on consumer goods, one's own sales force can be a prolific source of information. It is not uncommon to find on one's own payroll a great deal of untapped information which can help in the formulation of pricing policies.

Your own sales force are expert on competitors' pricing policies, product qualities and weaknesses, marketing and distribution strengths, and customer attitudes.

However, unless the feedback of this information is regularized, it will come in the form of a patchwork of individual comments of varying reliability. In most situations, older information will be quickly forgotten and only the most recent encounter will be in the forefront of the salesman's mind.

The way to organize this source of information is to emulate the approach of military intelligence, which is to collect detailed information from all sources, and then to find out whether a pattern emerges.

In practical terms, this means setting up a system of files to contain information on competition. Information to be recorded would include the following.

Pricing policies
Product range
Product performance and quality
Type of customer
Customer service
Distribution facilities
Sales force management
General management style
Customer attitudes
Cost structure

All information gathered from technical publications, exhibitions, customers, distribution, filed accounts, and from the purchase and study of products should be included in these files. From the files, a meaningful pattern will emerge. It will become possible to predict that if Company A increases prices, Company B will follow within a few weeks, whereas Company C will make no changes. It will become obvious which companies and which products are highly thought of by customers, and which hold their own by aggressive pricing. The information gathered will become an essential background to pricing decisions.

There is perhaps one danger in establishing an information system of this kind. A sales force can be an unreliable source of information on competitors' prices, because buyers have a strong motivation to understate these when talking to salesmen from other companies. They may claim to be able to buy more cheaply just to bluff their way to a price reduction. It is a good idea to ask yourself the following questions:

1. Which salesman reported the price? What kind of man is he?
2. Is he more interested in commission, and would he look for an easy sell for the sake of that commission?
3. Is he a selective salesman who believes he is selling the best kind of work for his company?
4. Is his report the only one? Are there corroborating results?
5. Is the buyer 'fishing' for information usable against other suppliers to drive down prices?
6. Is the competitor's price lower on one specific product, to one particular customer, or is it part of a general price reduction?

All this is part of the science and the art, the information and the skill, the calculation and the judgement that go into effective pricing.

Profit planning
Getting the best prices one can does not necessarily, of itself, ensure profitability.

Profits come from balancing

Prices
Costs
Volumes
Product mix

Orders and products differ widely in volume, cost, price, and profit. Not all products yield the same profits, or place the same demands on facilities and capital available.

Orders can differ, also, in terms of

Type of product
Countries sold to
Type of customer outlet
Channels of distribution used

It is not always possible to realize the same profit on every sale of the same article. One can be sold locally, another can be sold abroad, through an agent, and may have to be flown out to the customer (see example on page 31).

Thus profit is not a single-valued function of time or quantity, but is rather composed of a number of pooled segments, from which a net profit ultimately develops.

These sources, or segments, of profit are important from the viewpoint of evaluating a company's strengths or weakness.

In profit-effective pricing, management must have a means of knowing the relative contribution which each segment makes to the profit structure in order to strike a proper balance among prices, product mix, volumes, and costs.

Pricing and profit planning therefore are coordinated exercises in which management analyses the various economic and strategic alternatives and compares them with each other. It selects the one which appears to be the most advantageous in each pricing situation.

Because a selling price is 'what you can get for it', and because there are many factors which cannot be measured objectively, a pricing method cannot be formalized. The dangers of rigid application of inflexible pricing formulae were discussed in the earlier chapters. Fortunately, it is possible to have a more rational approach to pricing and one which will meet the profit planning requirements.

Profit planning must take into consideration where an article may be sold. If a company pursues a universal selling price policy, no matter where the article is sold, then the resultant contribution to profit can be substantially different for the same articles—if, for example, they are sold to countries with differing trading terms for discounts and commissions, etc., or different freight costs.

On the other hand, if a company desires the same contribution for the same article no matter where it is sold, then it is a simple matter to calculate what the various prices should be.

In Fig. 5.6, the first part of the example illustrates the differing contributions resulting from the same selling prices, while the second part illustrates what selling prices are necessary to yield the same contributions.

Country	Germany		France		UK	
Selling price		£100.00		£100.00		£100.00
Variable order costs						
Discount	5.00		3.00		3.00	
Commission	7.50		7.50		5.00	
Freight (if any)	3.00		3.00		1.00	
Variable product costs						
Materials	20.00		20.00		20.00	
Conversion	25.00		25.00		25.00	
		60.50		55.50		54.00
CONTRIBUTION		£39.50		£41.50		£46.00

At what price should the product be sold abroad to yield the same contribution per unit as in the UK?

Calculation	Germany	France	UK
Contribution	46.00	46.00	46.00
plus Unit variable costs (Materials, conversion, and freight)	48.00	48.00	46.00
Gross-up to allow for discounts and commission	94.00 $\times \dfrac{100}{87\frac{1}{2}}$	94.00 $\times \dfrac{100}{89\frac{1}{2}}$	92.00 $\times \dfrac{100}{92}$
NEW SELLING PRICE NEEDED	= 107.50	= 105.00	= 100.00
Proof			
Deduct discount and commission	(12½% of 107.50) 13.50	(10½% of 105) 11.00	(8% of 110) 8.00
	94.00	94.00	92.00
less Unit variable costs	48.00	48.00	46.00
Common contributions	46.00	46.00	46.00

Fig. 5.6. Contribution to profit by product sold in different countries

6

A rational approach to pricing

The contribution approach to more profitable pricing

In developing a more rational approach to pricing, it should be recognized that

1. Pricing decisions involve more than the use of traditional cost-plus methods in setting asking prices for products offered to customers.
2. Pricing is a market-oriented exercise and, more often than not, the pricing decision to be made is whether or not to meet a competitive or market price. In these circumstances, price-setting has given way to measuring the economic benefits to the seller of meeting a competitive price.
3. To measure these economic benefits needs a knowledge of those costs which are directly entailed by filling an order.

Every order a company obtains means a change in its expenses. To fulfil a specific order, a company must acquire the materials to be used in that order, and pay for the labour that will go into the materials. In addition, it will incur expenses for packing and shipping, and will also pay sales commission and discount on the order.

These are the out-of-pocket costs which are linked with filling the order. They are variable costs, which will rise and fall according to the level of activity, and which are avoidable if activity falls off.

Any excess of the selling price over the variable costs goes towards meeting the other expenses of the company, the fixed expenses. In other words, it yields a *contribution* (see Fig. 6.1).

Selling price	× × ×
less Variable costs	× ×
= CONTRIBUTION	× ×

Fig. 6.1. A product's contribution towards meeting fixed expenses

When the aggregate of contributions from all orders is more than enough to meet the fixed expenses, a profit results.

Imagine a pool, like the one in Fig. 6.2, with levels marked up the inside representing fixed expenses, break-even, and target profit. Pour in water until it reaches the fixed expenses level. If one imagines the contribution from each type of product as a stone, and the appropriate quantity of stones of the appropriate size are dropped into the pool, one should see the water level rise progressively above the fixed expense level, up to the break-even level, and, if there are enough stones, up to and beyond the target profit level.

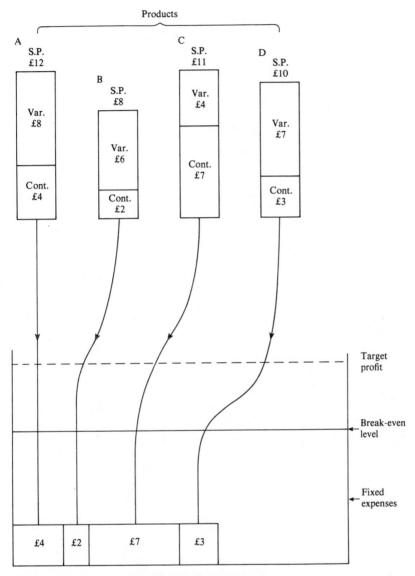

Fig. 6.2. The contribution pool

By considering the contribution of each product, we get a much more objective view of the value of the product price to the company. We look, in other words, at how much of each selling price is left, after deducting the variable costs, to contribute to the fixed expenses and profit.

Let us consider a clothing factory, for example. If we accept that the availability of sewing room labour is the factor that governs the output of a making-up shop, and if the contribution of each product is expressed in terms of its use of sewing room labour, then we can compare the relative value to the

Product	Selling price	'Full' cost	Net profit	per cent	Variable costs	Contribution	Use of facility (sewing room hours)	Contribution per hour
(a)	(b)	(c)	(d) = (b) − (c)	(e)	(f)	(g) = (b) − (f)	(h)	(i) = (g) ÷ (h)
	£	£	£		£	£	Hours	£
X	100	90	10	10%	50	50	10	5.00
Y	80	72	8	10%	45	35	3½	10.00
Z	60	54	6	10%	20	40	5	8.00
							Stage 1	Stage 2

Apparent order of profitability: Stage 1—All equally profitable.
Stage 2—Y, Z, X.

Fig. 6.3. The changing view on profitability

company of each product by its contribution per hour, as in Fig. 6.3. According to the traditional formulae, X, Y, and Z all seem equally profitable (Stage 1), but this is by no means so once contribution per hour is taken into account (Stage 2). Note also that, where salesmen are remunerated by commission, 25 per cent more would be paid for X than for Y. Yet the value of Y to the company per hour is twice that of X.

If the limit of available capacity is, say, 1000 hours per week, then the largest aggregate profit would be obtained if one selected first the products with the highest contribution yield per hour, then those with the next highest yield per hour, and so on.

It would be idle to pretend that one could drop all the less profitable products and make only the more profitable ones. Customers still expect to see a balanced range, but when one can see the facts so objectively it concentrates the mind wonderfully on which products are most profitable. It also indicates those products which require a price lift, and it permits the selection of a more gainful product mix.

Chapter 7 shows how to apply this concept of contribution per hour to building up prices and making pricing decisions.

7

Mechanics of installing a rational pricing programme

How much profit?

To businesses struggling against inflation, this question may seem somewhat academic. The fact remains, however, that a business cannot survive in the long term without making profits. Planning must be aimed at moving the business into a position where it can both be and remain profitable.

Before one can answer the question of what is an adequate profit, a further question arises of how one should judge adequacy and how it should be expressed.

If one accepts that profit is the reward of capital, a proper index of success should relate the results of operating to the facilities and resources used to achieve those results. In financial terms, net profits should be expressed as a return on the capital employed in the business.

Probably the most helpful approach is to use ratios to show the inter-relationships between vital financial aspects of the business. Such ratios help us view profitability as a measure of the use of resources, rather than concentrating on absolute profit, which may in certain circumstances be dangerously misleading.

The main, or primary, ratio to be considered is:

$$\frac{\text{Net profit}}{\text{Capital employed}}$$

This ratio shows the rate of return on the total capital employed in the business and comprises two other ratios:

$$\frac{\text{Net profit}}{\text{Sales}} \quad \text{and} \quad \frac{\text{Sales}}{\text{Capital employed}}$$
$$\text{(Profit margin)} \qquad \text{(Capital turnover)}$$

The derivation of these and other ratios can be seen in Fig. 7.1, a strategic profit model.

It will be seen from the above that an unchanged return on capital employed could result from a lower profit margin and a higher rate of capital turnover. Similarly a constant profit-to-sales ratio plus an increased turnover of capital employed would result in a higher rate of return. The interaction of these two factors is one of the keys to profitability.

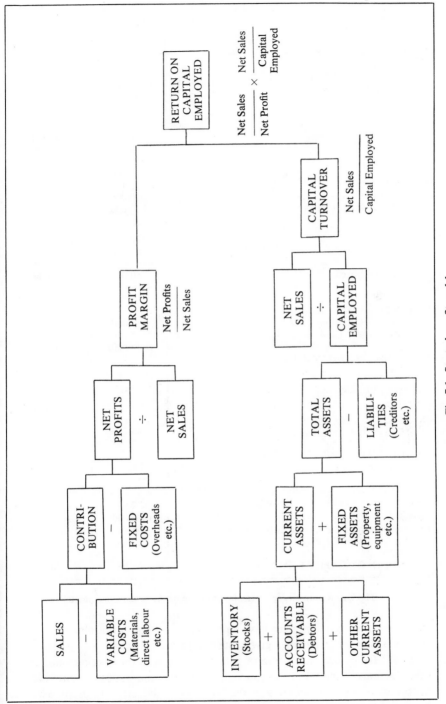

Fig. 7.1. Strategic profit model

	Company A (owns its fixed assets)	Company B (leases its fixed assets)
(a) Fixed assets		
Land and buildings (deprec. 2½% p.a.)	£50 000	—
Machinery (deprec. 10% p.a.)	50 000	—
	100 000	—
(b) Current assets		
Stocks	100 000	100 000
Debtors	80 000	80 000
	180 000	180 000
(c) Current liabilities		
Creditors	70 000	70 000
Overdraft (12% int. p.a.)	50 000	—
	120 000	70 000
(d) Net current assets (b) − (c)	60 000	110 000
(e) Capital employed (a) + (d)	£160 000	£110 000
Profit		
Before depreciation	50 000	50 000
Depreciation (land and buildings)	(1 250)	—
(machinery)	(5 000)	—
Rental (land and buildings)		(5 000) Assume (10% of cost)
Rental (machinery)	—	(10 000) Assume (20% of cost)
(f) NET PROFIT (pre-tax)	£43 750	£35 000
(g) RETURN ON CAPITAL EMPLOYED (%) (f) ÷ (e) × 100	25.3%	31.8%

Note In Company A, Interest on overdraft is left out of the calculation of return on capital employed as it is a finance cost rather than an operating cost.

	Company A	Company B
(h) Sales	£400 000	£400 000
(i) Profit as percentage of turnover (f) ÷ (h) × 100	10.9%	8.75%
(j) NO. OF TIMES CAPITAL TURNED OVER (h) × (i)	2.5 times	3.6 times
(k) RETURN ON CAPITAL EMPLOYED (i) × (j)	27.3%	31.8%

Fig. 7.2. Return on capital employed for Company A and Company B

These ratios by themselves have some value and any profit plan must be in essence a plan for achieving a given rate of return.

It can also be useful to compare a firm's ratios with those being achieved in other sections of the business or industry. But it is important to ensure that the figures used by other sections of the business or industry are prepared on a consistent basis, or the results may be misleading rather than helpful. And too much reliance ought not to be placed on inter-firm comparisons, which may at best give an average performance for a number of imperfect businesses.

Capital employed to sustain the same level of business can vary considerably, as the example in Fig. 7.2 shows. As a consequence, there can be a significant difference in the return on capital employed.

In calculating the amount of capital employed necessary to sustain an anticipated level of business, priority should be given to the day-to-day needs of working capital to keep operations flowing. That is, what funds are needed to buy raw materials, to finance debtors, etc., after taking account of relief obtained from suppliers in the form of credit. In a period of inflation, the amount of working capital needed to service the same quantity of business is ever-increasing. A bolt of cloth may cost £100 at the beginning of the year but need £120 to replace at the end of the year. Although £20 extra working capital is needed, we still have only one bolt of cloth. Similarly, inflationary prices mean higher values though not necessarily higher quantities of debtors and work in progress.

It is only when the growing needs of working capital are met that one should consider how to finance the fixed assets. It is little use having most of one's capital tied up in fixed assets (such as land, buildings, machinery, cars, etc.) if there is too little cash left to maintain a steady flow of materials needed for production.

To quote a phrase: 'Assets are for earning, not necessarily for owning.'

Examination of some manufacturing companies' Balance Sheets could give the impression that they were in the property business, not manufacturing.

In deciding what percentage return on capital employed is necessary, by all means take a guide from the information afforded by inter-firm comparisons. But the most satisfactory calculation of adequacy is probably that synthesized within one's own company.

What do we want the return to do? It has to satisfy three requirements:

1. It should give reasonable satisfaction to stockholders, who are risking capital.
2. It should contain an element to finance normal growth.
3. It should contain an element to counter the effects of inflation.

It could well be that, after due consideration, the board decide that their target requirements should be as follows:

> 10% to give reasonable stockholder satisfaction
> 5% to finance normal growth, and
> 10% to counter the effects of inflation
> ———
> 25% p.a. on capital employed
> ———

If corporation tax is 52 per cent, then the pre-tax target return must be

$$\frac{25}{(100-52)} \times 100 = 52.08\% \text{ on capital employed.}$$

What this amounts to, as a percentage on sales, depends on the rate of capital turnover. If, for instance, this was four times a year, then the target return would be $(52.08 \div 4) = 13$ per cent on sales.

In making the provision to offset the effects of inflation, reference should be made to the current tax relief available on increases in inventory values.

Having decided what profit is desired, we can now proceed with the mechanics of installing the rational pricing programme.

Recognizing the limiting (or key) factor

How does one recognize the limiting (or key) factor?

First, we should define what it is we are seeking:

'*The limiting (or key) factor* is that part of the production process which is not readily expandable, but through which all products must pass. The overall level of output is thereby limited to what that process can handle.'

In most industrial situations, the limiting factor is time. It may be the available hours of skilled labour, or the operating hours of a piece of process plant. In non-industrial situations, it can be some other factor, such as selling space in a retail store.

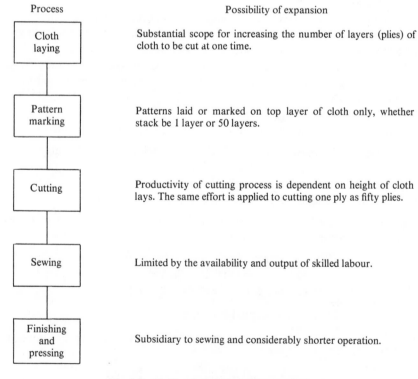

Process	Possibility of expansion
Cloth laying	Substantial scope for increasing the number of layers (plies) of cloth to be cut at one time.
Pattern marking	Patterns laid or marked on top layer of cloth only, whether stack be 1 layer or 50 layers.
Cutting	Productivity of cutting process is dependent on height of cloth lays. The same effort is applied to cutting one ply as fifty plies.
Sewing	Limited by the availability and output of skilled labour.
Finishing and pressing	Subsidiary to sewing and considerably shorter operation.

Fig. 7.3. Limiting factor for clothing company

To decide which is the limiting factor, one should prepare a diagram of the sequence of operations, and against each operation should be an appraisal of how readily the productive capacity of that operation could be expanded.

The process or operation with the least possibility of ready expansion is the limiting (or key) factor.

Examples
Let us look at the limiting factor for a clothing company (Fig. 7.3), a processing plant (Fig. 7.4), and a retail outlet (Fig. 7.5). It is clear from examining Fig. 7.3, that, in the clothing company, the sewing process is that which regulates the ultimate output. The possibility of expansion depends on the availability of labour, the capacity and length of time to train, and the space to accommodate the increased numbers.

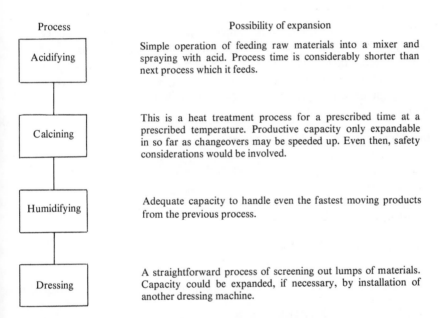

Fig. 7.4. Limiting factor for processing industry

Figure 7.4, based on a company in the processing industry, shows that the key factor which limits throughput is calcining time. With space and finance it would be possible, of course, to expand the productive capacity by building more plant. However, one should always consider the permanence of any increased demand and the effect on the market of extra capacity within the industry.

In the retailing example, shown in Fig. 7.5, it is obvious that the major limiting factor is space for display and sale, with a possible secondary limiting factor of finance to sustain stock levels.

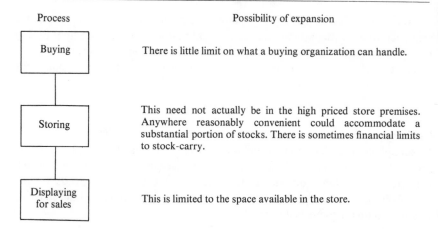

Process	Possibility of expansion
Buying	There is little limit on what a buying organization can handle.
Storing	This need not actually be in the high priced store premises. Anywhere reasonably convenient could accommodate a substantial portion of stocks. There is sometimes financial limits to stock-carry.
Displaying for sales	This is limited to the space available in the store.

Fig. 7.5. Limiting factor for a retail outlet

While not all situations are as simple as those in the examples above, it is usually possible, after sufficient examination, to identify the limiting factor.

The limiting factor sometimes changes temporarily. For instance, in a time of materials rationing or shortage, the availability of materials can become the limiting factor where previously it might have been the availability of skilled labour.

Installing a rational pricing programme

Having considered the desired return on capital employed and identified the limiting factor, the first step in installing the pricing programme is to calculate the target for contributions.

1. Target contributions for year

This is calculated in the following way:

Fixed expenses (per budget)	say	£70 050
Desired profit (% on sales or % on capital employed)	say	£20 000
TARGET FOR CONTRIBUTIONS		£90 150

2. Units of limiting factor

The second step is to be realistic about the number of effective sewing room hours (the limiting factor) we have for sale. Of a nominal capacity of 83 200 hours, only 48 730 effective hours are for sale, as the calculation below shows:

(a) Nominal capacity = 40 employees × 260 days 8 hr per day = 83 200
(b) Reduce for holidays = 40 employees × 235 days 8 hr per day = 75 200
(c) Reduce by absenteeism, say 10% = 67 680
(d) Apply average percentage utilization, say 80% = 54 144

(e) Apply average performance, say 90% = 48 730

3. *Target contribution per hour*

The next step is to divide the target contributions by the available sewing room hours, to arrive at a target contribution per hour.

$$\frac{\text{Target £}}{\text{Saleable hours}} = \frac{£90\ 150}{48\ 730} = £1.85$$

2 (Revised). *Units of limiting factor*

It should be noted that in calculating the units of the limiting factor in step 2, how slight improvements in the percentages of absenteeism, utilization, and performance can have a significant cumulative effect on the units available.

If, for instance, absenteeism was 8 per cent instead of 10 per cent; utilization was 85 per cent instead of 80 per cent; and performance was 95 per cent instead of 90 per cent, then the units of the limiting factor available would be as follows:

(a) Nominal capacity (hr)	83 200
(b) Reduce for holidays	75 200
(c) Reduce for absenteeism 8%	69 184
(d) Apply percentage utilization 85%	58 806
(e) Apply percentage performance 95%	55 866

Thus there would be 55 866 hours available against 48 730 hours previously, a 14.6 per cent increase.

However, one must be realistic, and if no effective effort is planned or made to improve absenteeism, utilization, and performance, one cannot expect the percentages to improve in this way.

4. *Product cost build-up sheet*

The last step is to make out a product cost build-up sheet (shown in Fig. 7.6) which records all the appropriate variable costs, for example:

Piece goods
Trimmings, etc.
Labour
Packing and delivery

and also those variable costs that are based on the ultimate price, for example

Sales commission
Cash discount

The most interesting features of this form are the two boxes at the foot. The one on the left shows how to build up to a target price—i.e., the 'asking' price. The box on the right starts with the market price and works backwards to see if the contribution per hour is acceptable.

Item	Two-piece suit		Lot No. M214		Season: Spring 1974	
Line	Category	Item	Quantity (yards)	Price	Cost per dozen each	
		DESCRIPTION				
a	Piece goods		3.25	£2.00	6.50	
b						
c		Freight on pce. goods				
		DESCRIPTION				
d		Pocketing				
e		Linings or banding				
f	Linings and	Zippers				
g	trimmings	Thread				
h		Other trim				
i		Total: linings & trim			1.75	
		Cost centre	S.A.H.	Rate	Cost excesses	
j		Cutting	1.0	55p	0.55 10%	0.055	0.605
k	Direct labour	Sewing	5.0	45p	2.25 12%	0.27	2.52
l		Finishing	1.0	50p	0.50 10%	0.05	0.55
m						
n	Other variable	Delivery charges			0.25	
o	costs (product-based)	Packing materials			0.15	
p		etc.				
q	TOTAL VARIABLE COSTS (product-based)				12.325	
r	Variable costs	Cash discount		3%		
s	(price-based)	Sales commission		5%		
t						
u		TOTAL %		8%		

TARGET SELLING PRICE & CONTRIBUTION			ACTUAL SELLING PRICE & CONTRIBUTION	
Variable cost (product-based)		12.325	Selling price	20.00
(line q)			less Variable costs:	
add Target contribution:			(line q)	12.325
C.p.h. £1.85 × 5 hrs		9.25	(line u) i.e. 8% of S.P.	1.600
	(92%)	21.575	Contribution	6.075
Variable cost (price-based)	(8%)	1.874	Sewing room hours	5
TARGET PRICE	(100%)	£23.429	CONTRIBUTION PER HOUR	£1.213

Fig. 7.6. Product cost build-up sheet

The benefits from a rational pricing programme

Contribution requires only that the variable (or out-of-pocket) costs and the selling price be known. Adding an allocation of fixed cost only distorts the objectivity of any comparison and could lead management into making wrong decisions.

The aim of the rational pricing programme is to achieve the most favourable sales mix of products that will yield the highest aggregate contributions.

Of course, to be able to select the most profitable orders presupposes that there are enough orders from which to choose. When this is so, the improvement in profit can be dramatic.

Let us consider the record of inquiries shown in Fig. 7.7.

Inquiry no.	S.P.	Contribution	Sewing room hours required	C.p.h.
1235	£1,400	£350	140	£2.50
6	300	100	25	4.0
7	850	425	170	2.5
8	920	250	50	5.0
9	1,000	350	115	3.0
		1,475	500	
1240	741	317	100	3.2
1	150	50	30	1.67
2	537	200	60	3.33
3	85	40	8	5.0
4	2,000	500	50	10.0
5	2,208	736	92	8.0

Fig. 7.7. Chronological order bookings

If there were only 500 hours available, and the orders were accepted chronologically, only orders 1235/9 would be taken and the aggregate contributions would be £1475.

The contribution attainable if one were able to select the most profitable orders could be as shown in Fig. 7.8 below.

Inquiry	Contribution	Hours
1244	500	50
1245	736	92
1243	40	8
1238	250	50
1236	100	25
1242	200	60
1240	317	100
1239	350	115
	£2493	500 hours

Fig. 7.8. Most profitable selection of orders

When each order is evaluated as to its contribution content and its demands upon production facilities, it is possible to maintain a running record of the contribution content and use of facilities, such as that in Fig. 7.9.

Order no.	Contribution	Hours	C.p.h.	Cumulative		
				Cum. contribs	Cum. hours	Cum. c.p.h.
	TARGETS BREAK-EVEN		£90 150 pa £70 150 pa	£45 075 £35 075	24 365 hrs	£1.85
1	400	200	2.0	400	200	2.0
2	300	160	1.875	700	360	1.94
3	800	500	1.6	1 500	860	1.74
54	700	320	2.19	36 500	18 268	2.0
55	1 500	682	2.2	38 000	18 950	2.0
56	2 000	1 050	1.9	40 000	20 000	2.0
			Not yet allocated	5 075	4 365	1.16

Fig. 7.9. Season contribution progress record (assuming season is half the year)

The effect of orders on the cumulative contribution per hour can be seen, and the extent to which targets are being achieved and production facilities occupied.

This gives management a very positive indication of the cumulative results of their efforts. Indications of profitability are provided as selling is proceeding, while there is still time to influence the results, rather than as a record of history compiled after the event.

Working out the contribution from each product makes it possible to get a reliable indication of the results of the factory's efforts each week, by multiplying the production by the appropriate contributions and deducting from the aggregate a week's proportion of the fixed expenses. Figure 7.10 shows a weekly profitability statement of this kind.

WEEKLY PROFITABILITY STATEMENT Week ending:			
Item	Volume produced	Contribution per lb/doz	Total contributions
26 L	50	£10	500
18 L	40	11.25	450
27 M	150	6	900
Total contributions			1850
* Weeks' budget of fixed overheads			1493
PROFIT (LOSS) ON WEEK			357

* Budget fixed expenses were £70 150 for 47 working weeks, i.e. £1493 per week.

Fig. 7.10. Weekly profitability statement

Such an indication of the week's results assumes, of course, that the production has not necessitated the use of more materials, more machine time, or more sewing room labour than envisaged when calculating the product contributions.

'Expectable' profits are 'expectable' in the sense that the variable costs that have been used in arriving at these results are estimates, and also that the level of fixed costs envisaged is only a budget.

If such a weekly profitability statement were being run in conjunction with standard costing, then the weekly operating variances could be applied to this indication of profitability as an additional refinement.

For a company wishing to further its control of the business, the next natural development would be the comparison of actual costs with the 'standard' costs used in the pricing exercise, and the measurement and comparison of actual fixed costs with those budgeted in the setting of target contributions. Such a development is considered in the next chapter.

Summary

Let us now sum up the benefits of a rational pricing programme. It provides:

1. A method of price build-up that is undistorted by arbitrary allocations of overhead expenses. In a multi-product, multi-process, multi-market business, the absorption of fixed overheads in individual product costs is completely arbitrary.
2. A reliable guide as to just how acceptable a market price is to the company.
3. An objective comparison of the relative worth of each product to the company.
4. A reliable indication, while selling is in progress, of the extent to which targets of profitability and utilization of capacity are being achieved.
5. The ability to provide a weekly profit and loss statement.

Cost control

The basic premise on which both standard costing and budgetary control are founded is the view that the important factor is what a product or function can reasonably be planned to cost, rather than what it actually cost on a previous occasion of manufacture.

It is considered that this approach is beneficial to use both when considering selling prices and for measuring the efficiency of the business.

The selling prices developed on cost sheets are based on a standard usage of materials and labour, standard costs of packaging, and delivery charges. If the contributions indicated on the cost sheets are to be achieved, costs must be kept in line with these standards.

The fixed costs we are aiming to recover as part of the target contributions are budgeted fixed costs. It is equally important that these, too, should be kept in line with the budget of fixed costs.

The control of these costs is effected by:

1. Establishing target costs (known as *standard*, as far as materials, labour, and other variable costs are concerned, and the *budget*, as far as overhead costs are concerned).
2. Ascertaining and measuring actual performance or costs.
3. Comparing *actual* performance or costs with the *standard* (or *budget*).
4. Calculating and interpreting any variances.
5. Taking any necessary remedial action to eliminate the causes of the variances.

The way to achieve this kind of control is through preparing a *weekly production summary* on the use of labour and materials and achievement of target contributions. Such a summary is shown in Fig. 7.11. Poor performance in some respect should show up when the weekly summary is examined.

		9009	2143 blouse	2157 blouse					TOTAL	£
VOLUME (a)	GARMENT TYPE	9009	2143 blouse	2157 blouse						
(b)	OUTPUT (dozens)	140	160	70					370	
(c)	Selling price per dozen	22.00	15.00	16.00						
(d)	TOTAL SALES VALUE (b) × (c)	3080	2400	1120						6600
MATERIALS (e)	Materials—cost per dozen	6.28	2.82	3.00						
(f)	TOTAL MATERIALS (b) × (c)	879	453	210						1542
(g)	Actual materials used	850	500	240						
(h)	VARIANCE (f) − (g)	29	(47)	(30)						(48)
LABOUR (i)	Attended hours								1200	
(j)	Budgeted labour efficiency								0.80	
(k)	Expected machining hours produced (i) × (j)								960	
(l)	Budgeted contribution p. hr								4.00	
LABOUR (m)	EXPECTED CONTRIBUTIONS (k) × (l)									£3840
(n)	Machining hours per dozen	2.54	2.08	2.15						
(o)	TOTAL MACHINING HOURS PRODUCED (b) × (n)	356	333	151					840	
(p)	Actual labour efficiency (o) ÷ (i)								0.70	
(q)	Machining cost per dozen	3.175	2.60	2.6875						
(r)	TOTAL MACHINING WAGES EARNED (b) × (q)	445	416	189						
CONTRIBUTIONS (s)	BUDGETED CONTRIBUTION VALUE OF M/C HRS EARNED (l) × (o)	1424	1332	604						£3360
(t)	Contributions per dozen	10.0	8.0	9.0						
(u)	CONTRIBUTIONS EARNED (b) × (t)	1400	1280	630						£3310
CONTRIBUTIONS (v)	Efficiency variance (m) − (s)								(480)	
(w)	Mixture variance (s) − (u)								(50)	
(x)	Wages paid								1450	
(y)	Attended hrs × std. rate								1200	
(z)	LABOUR RATE VARIANCE (x) − (y)									(250)
(aa)	MATERIALS VARIANCE (h)									(48)
(bb)	ACTUAL CONTRIBUTIONS (u) − (z) − (aa)									£3012

Fig. 7.11. Weekly production summary

THIS MONTH			EXPENSE		MONTHS TO DATE		
Budget	Actual	Variance	Code no.	Description	Budget	Actual	Variance
			Controllable expenses: Indirect labour National Insurance Company pension scheme Repairs Consumable stores Misc. supplies Water Gas Electricity Fuel oil				
		%	TOTAL CONTROLLABLE % Actual of budget				%
			Non-controllable expenses Rent Rates Depreciation TOTAL NON-CONTROLLABLE				
			TOTAL OVERHEAD EXPENSES				

Factory/Department: *Month ending:*

Expected contributions (m)	Efficiency variance (v)	Mixture variance (w)	Labour rate variance (z)	Materials variance (aa)	Actual contributions (bb)	Week ending
						Total this period
						Total previous period
						Total to date

Comment:

Fig. 7.12. Operating statement

Cost centre:				Month ending:			
THIS MONTH			EXPENSE		MONTHS TO DATE		
Budget	Actual	Variance	Code no.	Description	Budget	Actual	Variance

Fig. 7.13. Monthly operating statement

The weekly production summary illustrated is in use in an important and successful clothing manufacturers, and is designed to report the quantities of each garment produced, and evaluate the garments produced into:

Sales value
Standard materials' usage
Standard machining hours earned
Standard machining wages earned
Contributions earned

It contrasts the four latter with the actual performance, evaluating any variance in money terms.

It contrasts the contributions earned with those budgeted, and permits the recognition of how much of the variance between contributions expected and actual contributions is due to product mix, labour efficiency, labour rates, and materials cost.

To keep a cumulative production summary, it is only necessary to accumulate actual production, attended hours, wages paid, and materials used; all the other figures can be calculated from these.

Each factory or department should prepare each month an *operating statement* (see Fig. 7.12), set out in two parts. Part 1 shows the budgeted and actual expenses appropriate to that factory or department during the month, together with cumulative figures for the months to date. Part 2 gives a week-by-week record of expected contributions, efficiency variance, mixture variance, labour rate variance, and materials variance, netting down to the actual contributions. When the total of the four or five weeks in the current period is added to the previous cumulative total, a new cumulative total inclusive of the current period is derived.

PROFIT SUMMARY

Month:	*Expected contributions*	*Actual contributions*	
Production departments			
1.			
2.			
3.			
4.			
Service departments			
Administration			
Marketing			
Personnel			
PROFIT FOR MONTH			

Fig. 7.14. Profit summary

51

For all the other non-producing cost centres a monthly operating statement (see Fig. 7.13) is prepared.

Thereafter, all the operating statements can be summarized on a *profit summary*, like the one shown in Fig. 7.14.

Such a summary can also be produced on a cumulative basis.

By this relatively simple control process, the extent to which actual costs and performances have been kept in line with those estimated at the time selling prices were arranged can be measured.

Many manufacturers try to run their business with only the conventional profit and loss statement to guide them, and would be faced with something like Fig. 7.15.

Invoiced sales	£100 000
Material costs	20 000
Direct labour	30 000
Factory overheads	25 000
Gen. and administrative overheads	15 000
TOTAL COST	£90 000
PRE-TAX PROFITS	£10 000

Fig. 7.15. Conventional profit and loss statement

Invoiced sales		£100 000
Expected variable costs		70 000
EXPECTED CONTRIBUTION		30 000
Mixture variance		5 000
Operating variances		
Materials		(1 200)
Efficiency		(8 000)
Labour rate		(800)
ACTUAL CONTRIBUTION		25 000
less Fixed costs		
Budget	15 000	
Variance	nil	
		15 000
PRE-TAX PROFIT		10 000
Target profit		15 000
Profit variance		(5 000)

Fig. 7.16. Contribution statement

If the target profit was £15 000, then there is a shortfall of £5000. Why?

Is it that the prices have been wrong?
> or

Has marketing concentrated on the less profitable lines?
> or

Have there been operating inefficiencies?
> or

Has there been over-spending?

How much more favourably equipped he would be to make better quality decisions if the same result were presented in the more meaningful way possible under the rational pricing method—see Fig. 7.16.

The manufacturer is now able to see why his profits are £5000 less than expected.

He is able to see that there is a variance of £5000 arising out of a more favourable product mix. But this is more than offset by (£10 000) of unfavourable operating variances.

He can see clearly where action is needed, and once the problem is identified it is halfway to being solved.

Use of basic data for other managerial decisions

Use of rational approach in order acceptance decisions
Compare this more rational approach with the rigid adherence to questionable cost-plus pricing formulae, which can often mean not accepting business which could have been profitable.

Such an example is shown in Fig. 8.1.

Work taken	Product lines			Annual total
	L	*M*	*N*	
Formula S.P.	100 000	40 000	80 000	220 000
Variable costs	30 000	10 000	25 000	65 000
Contribution	70 000	30 000	55 000	155 000
Per cent	70	75	68.75	
less Fixed costs				200 000
OPERATING LOSS				(45 000)
Work turned down *(because it failed to sell at formula prices)*	*O*	*P*	*Q*	*Total*
Formula S.P.	70 000	50 000	40 000	160 000
Actual S.P. available	60 000	45 000	30 000	135 000
Variable cost	20 000	18 000	10 000	48 000
CONTRIBUTION	40 000	27 000	20 000	87 000
Per cent	57	54	50	

Fig. 8.1. The effects of strict cost-plus pricing when there is under-used capacity

Such a situation, if there was under-used capacity capable of taking O, P, and/or Q, could have earned £87 000 more contribution and have turned a loss on the work taken (of £45 000) into a profit of £42 000 (87 000 − 45 000).

Obviously, in filling up capacity by accepting whatever prices are available (always assuming they are in excess of variable costs), one should be careful not to jeopardize one's regular full-price business. This is sometimes possible by placing the lower-priced business outside the normal market. If this is not possible, different labels might be considered, or even making for the customer's own label.

Critics of pricing techniques based on the contribution concept claim that there is a danger that everything will be priced below its 'real' cost—i.e., the cost including an absorption of fixed overheads—and so the company can be operating at a loss although all products are making some contribution. This is certainly possible, but if the volume of sales is inadequate, a company can be making a loss just as easily when pricing on an absorption costing basis. Both systems require monitoring, either of volume or of total contribution. Companies can misuse either system, but, in most situations, pricing decisions made on the contribution concept are more likely to be correct, in their influence on total profitability, than decisions based on 'total' cost.

There are other benefits arising out of the use of the contribution concept as a foundation for pricing policies.

1. It helps to fill capacity and therefore improve profitability in times of intensive competition.
2. While absorption costing is a rigid system, the contribution method enables manufacturers to be more aggressive in their pricing policy.
3. The crucial advantage is that it focuses attention on market pricing. It takes explicit account of the price/volume relationship. The unavoidable corollary is that it requires thought and judgement rather than just following a formula.

Sales incentive scheme

Part 1. The general case

The traditional sales incentive scheme takes the form of paying the salesman a commission, calculated as a percentage of the sales revenue booked by him. This is sometimes combined with a flat basic salary, or it may be that the salesman is rewarded solely by a commission on sales. In some schemes, the manufacturer will pay different rates of commission on different product lines, usually based on the profits supposedly generated by the various products.

All these schemes may apply the percentage rates of commission to the whole sales revenue or only to that part of it that exceeds a certain target revenue.

These types of incentive schemes designed to generate sales revenue are often misplaced, and can actually have a bad effect on profits when the wrong kind of revenue occupies all the productive capacity of a company.

When a flat commission is paid on sales revenue, the company is implying that all sales revenue £s have the same value to the company. But, as we saw in earlier chapters, some sales £s may yield a higher benefit to the company than others.

It is worth reiterating why this is so.

Every order a salesman obtains brings with it certain expenses that will be directly incurred in the fulfilment of that order. For example, the company must acquire the *materials* to be used in that order, and pay the *labour* who will be working on these materials. In addition, it will incur expenses for *packing* and *shipping*. It may also pay *sales commission* and allow *cash discount* on that order.

These are the out-of-pocket, or variable, costs which are entailed by fulfilling the order. They are the avoidable costs if the order is not taken.

The value of the order to the company is the difference between the selling price obtained and these variable costs. This difference is called the *contribution*.

It is the contribution that the order makes to the fixed overheads and profits. When the aggregate of contributions from all orders is more than enough to meet the fixed overhead expenses, a profit results.

By considering the contribution of each product, we get a much more objective view of the value of the product price to the company, i.e., how much of each selling price is left, after deducting the out-of-pocket costs, to contribute to fixed expenses and profit.

Every manufacturer has some practical limit to his production facilities. If we accept, for instance, in the clothing industry, that the availability of sewing room labour is the factor that governs the output of a making-up shop, and if the contribution of each product is expressed in terms of its use of sewing room labour, then we can compare the relative value to the company of each product by its contribution per hour.

Figure 8.2 shows examples of the relative worth of various orders to a company.

If the limit of availability is, say, 7000 hours per week, then the largest aggregate profit would be obtained if one selected first the products with the highest contribution yield per hour of limiting factor, then those with the next highest yield per hour, and so on.

You can see that what would, by traditional formulae, all seem equally profitable (Stage 1) are by no means so when looked at objectively, and uncluttered with arbitrary allocations of overhead expenses (Stage 2).

Note that where salesmen are remunerated by a flat rate of commission, 25 per cent more would be paid for X than for Y. Yet the value of Y to the company per hour is twice that of X. If the total availability of sewing room hours were 7000, then to fill them with 700 units of Product X would contribute *£35 000* at a sales commission cost of *£3500* (at 5 per cent commission)—i.e., a net contribution of £31 500—whereas to fill the available capacity with 2000 units of Product Y would contribute *£70 000* at a sales commission cost of *£8000* (at 5 per cent commission)—i.e., a net contribution of £62 000. Therefore a sales incentive scheme geared to generate the sales of Product X in preference to, or even equal with, Product Y is definitely harmful to the company.

A company's profit performance in an operating period is measured by the total amount of contribution generated minus the period's fixed expenses. Thus, once the company is committed for its period fixed expenses, it has to generate contribution £s irrespective of the sales £s booked. If this is the case, the incentive emphasis should be placed where it will generate the greatest amount of contribution £s of the right quality. It is suggested that, where commissions paid are related to the contributions generated, the influence on profits could be

Product	Selling price £	'Full' cost £	Net profit £	Per cent	Variable costs (materials, labour, packing, delivery, etc.) £	Contribution £	Use of facility (sewing room) hours	Contribution per hour £
(a)	(b)	(c)	(d) = (b) − (c)	(e)	(f)	(g) = (b) − (f)	(h)	(i) = (g) ÷ (h)
X	100	90	10	10	50	50	10	5.00
Y	80	72	8	10	45	35	$3\frac{1}{2}$	10.00
Z	60	54	6	10	20	40	5	8.00

↑ Stage 1

↑ Stage 2

Fig. 8.2. The changing view on profitability

quite dramatic. More annual profits can be made on less sales without threatening the maximum capacity limits of the company or exceeding the working capital ability of the firm. Most important, the company is more able to direct its own product mix.

Every £1000 of contribution is not necessarily as valuable to the company as every other £1000. It depends on the hours of limiting factor (sewing room hours in the clothing factory) utilized in achieving that contribution. Because of this, in order to encourage the selection of the most profitable product mix (i.e., yielding the highest contribution per hour) the incentive should contain two elements. The first should encourage volume of contributions, and the second encourage the best quality of contributions, as shown in Part 2 below, which describes the stages in designing and applying such an incentive scheme.

Part 2. Its application
Stage 1 If your salesmen are to sell the products which are most profitable to the company, they must know which those products are.

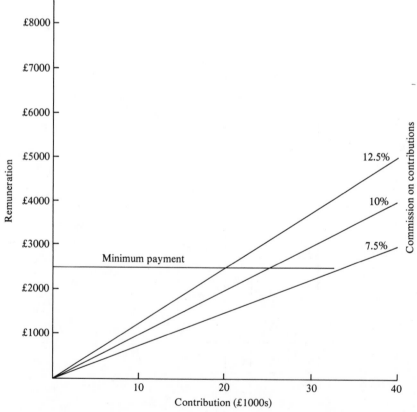

Fig. 8.3. **Percentage commission on all contributions, with a fall-back minimum payment of £2500**

It is, therefore, an essential requirement of the scheme that the contribution of each product and its use of the limiting factors be calculated, and a schedule prepared for use in conjunction with the scheme.

Where selling prices are determined by the manufacturer, the influence that the salesmen can exert is directed to the attainment of a more profitable product mix.

Stage 2   The proportion of a salesman's remuneration that is to be considered basic, and the proportion that is to be on incentive have to be decided.

From the company's point of view, if the incentive is considered a good one, then the bigger the proportion of total remuneration that is on incentive, the better for the company.

Although, initially, while the scheme is untried, a salesman may require some security, it could be a mistake to satisfy this need with a permanent high-base salary, and consequently low-value incentive. It would probably be better to run the new scheme alongside the old for a season, and pay out on the higher of the two.

Two approaches to this problem are shown in Figs. 8.3 and 8.4.

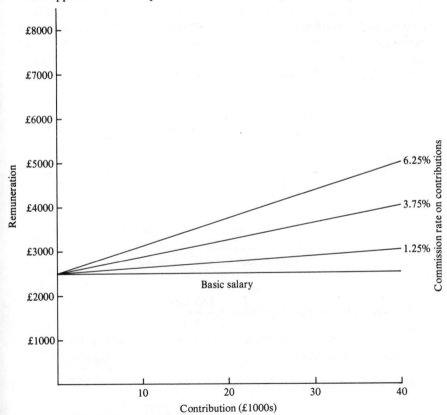

Fig. 8.4. Reduced percentage commission on all contributions, on top of a basic salary of £2500

Stage 3   The basic rate of commission for applying to the amount of contributions has to be determined.

What the right rate is for any specific company depends very much on what conditions are like in that particular industry, and what would attract a first-class salesman to do a first-class job.

Often, of course, the rate has to be fixed with some reference to what was available under the system being replaced.

Stage 4   By reference to the product cost sheets (see Fig. 7.6) the sales orders obtained should be evaluated as to their contribution content and the extent to which they will use the key facilities (i.e., the limiting factor).

By dividing the contribution content of his total orders by the hours' use of the limiting factor, an achieved contribution per hour will result.

Stage 5   To recognize the quality of contributions—i.e., what contribution per hour they represent—the basic rate of commission decided at Stage 3 should be adjusted in proportion to the ratio of the achieved contribution per hour to the target contribution per hour.

In this way, the salesmen will be encouraged to seek sales of the products yielding high contributions per hour, and the result could be a dramatic improvement in aggregate contributions, and hence ultimate net profits (see Figs. 8.5 and 8.6).

Figure 8.5 shows Salesman A's selling record.

| Product | Quantity | S.P. | Sales value £ | Contributions | | Hours | |
				Rate	Value £	Per unit	Total
X	500	100	50 000	50	25 000	10	5 000
Y	250	80	20 000	35	8 750	3½	875
Z	300	60	18 000	40	12 000	5	1 500
			88 000		45 750		7 375

Fig. 8.5. Sales record for Salesman A

A's achieved contribution per hour $= \dfrac{£45\ 750}{7375} = 6.2.$

Assume a target contribution of £8.0 per hour, and a basic rate of commission of 5 per cent.

Then commission payable to A would be: $5\% \times \dfrac{6.2}{8.0} \times £45\ 750$

$$= £1773$$

The record for Salesman B is shown in Fig. 8.6.

Product	Quantity	S.P.	Sales value £	Contributions		Hours	
				Rate	Value £	Per unit	Total
X	180	100	18 000	50	9 000	10	1 800
Y	500	80	70 000	35	17 500	3½	1 750
Z	500	60	30 000	40	20 000	5	2 500
			88 000		46 500		6 050

Fig. 8.6. Sales record for Salesman B

$$\text{B's achieved contribution per hour} = \frac{£46\ 500}{6050} = 7.7.$$

$$\text{Commission payable to B would be:} \quad 5\% \times \frac{7.7}{8.0} \times £46\ 500 = £2238$$

B gets 26 per cent more commission than A for selling the same sales turnover and substantially the same aggregate contributions, but his sales only occupy 6050 hours of limiting facility, whereas A's occupy 7375 hours. This enables 1325 hours to be filled by further productive and contribution earning work.

The use of the contribution concept to decide which goods to make in, and which to contract out

It is sometimes suggested that when a factory has ample opportunity to arrange for work to be contracted out, the concept of a limiting factor is non-effective. This is not so.

Let us consider the situation in a clothing factory once again. The sewing room hour will still be the limiting factor on production within a particular factory.

The introduction of the contracting-out capacity (or C.M.T., 'cut, make and trim', as it is known in the garment industry) only illustrates one further advantage that comes from the use of the contribution concept.

The target is still the highest aggregate of contributions. How this can be achieved when some garments are made outside can only be calculated by the contribution method.

The emphasis is now on which garments can most profitably be made outside to achieve the highest aggregate of contributions.

To determine this, the following method should be used.

1. Calculate a cost sheet for the garments made outside (see Fig. 8.7).
2. Next compare the contribution of company-made products with the contribution of C.M.T.-made products. Figure 8.8 gives an example of this calculation. One would, of course, expect the company-made garments to have a higher contribution. If not, what do we need the factory for?

Style	A	B	C	D
Materials	£4.00	£8.00	£5.00	£7.00
C.M.T. cost	£3.40	£7.40	£3.60	£9.73
Packing and delivery	£0.50	£0.50	£0.40	£0.60
Variable cost (Product-based)	£7.90	£15.90	£9.00	£17.33
Discount	$2\frac{1}{2}$%	$2\frac{1}{2}$%	$2\frac{1}{2}$%	$2\frac{1}{2}$%
Commission	5%	5%	5%	5%
Variable cost (price-based)	$7\frac{1}{2}$%	$7\frac{1}{2}$%	$7\frac{1}{2}$%	$7\frac{1}{2}$%
SELLING PRICE	£16.11	£19.35	£11.89	£23.06
less Variable cost (product-based)	£7.90	£15.90	£9.00	£17.33
less Variable cost (price-based)	£1.21	£1.45	£0.89	£1.73
= CONTRIBUTIONS	£7.00	£2.00	£2.00	£4.00
Order of profitability	1	3	3	2

Fig. 8.7. Contribution per style for garments made outside

Style	A	B	C	D
Materials	£4.00	£8.00	£5.00	£7.00
Sewing room labour (£1 per hour)	£2.00	£3.00	£1.20	£3.33
Other labour	£0.40	£0.40	£0.40	£0.40
Packing and delivery	£0.50	£0.50	£0.40	£0.60
Variable cost (product-based)	£6.90	£11.90	£7.0	£11.33
Discount	$2\frac{1}{2}$%	$2\frac{1}{2}$%	$2\frac{1}{2}$%	$2\frac{1}{2}$%
Commission	5%	5%	5%	5%
Variable cost (price-based)	$7\frac{1}{2}$%	$7\frac{1}{2}$%	$7\frac{1}{2}$%	$7\frac{1}{2}$%
SELLING PRICE	£16.11	£19.35	£11.89	£23.06
less Variable cost (product-based)	£6.90	£11.90	£7.00	£11.33
less Variable cost (price-based)	£1.21	£1.45	£0.89	£1.73
= CONTRIBUTION	£8.00	£6.00	£4.00	£10.00
÷ Making time (sewing room hours)	2	3	1.2	3.33
= CONTRIBUTION PER SEWING ROOM HOUR	£4.00	£2.00	£3.33	£3.00
Order of profitability	1	4	2	3

Fig. 8.8. Contribution and contribution per hour for garments made in own factory

3. The contribution advantage of each style should be measured against the making time, and a contribution advantage per hour (c.a.p.h.) calculated, as in Fig. 8.9.

4. The styles with the highest c.a.p.h. are the ones that should be made in the factory, and the ones with the lowest c.a.p.h. should be given out.

Style	Factory made (a)	C.M.T. made (b)	Contribs. advantage (c) = £(a) — (b)	Making time (d)	c.a.p.h. (c) ÷ (d)
A	8	7	1	2	0.50
B	6	2	4	3	1.33
C	4	2	2	1.2	1.67
D	10	4	6	$3\frac{1}{3}$	1.80
Order of precedence: D, C, B, A.					

Fig. 8.9. Comparison of contributions for garments made in own factory with those made outside

The order of precedence is not necessarily that which obtains before the introduction of C.M.T.

All other considerations being satisfactory (i.e., quality, delivery, etc.), the ones that should be made outside are:

A which is the style with the best contributions when made outside
and
B where the contribution advantage per hour when made in the factory is less than for C and D.

D and C should be made in the factory because their C.M.T. contributions are poorer than the factory made styles, and their contribution advantages per hour when made in the factory are higher than the other styles.

Normally, one would fill the factory before giving anything out, as the cost of unused capacity is likely to eliminate any contribution obtained from C.M.T.

Test
Assume the factory capacity is 5000 sewing room hours and the order book is as shown in Fig. 8.10.

Style	Units	S/R hrs per unit	Hours required
A	500	2	1000
B	600	3	1800
C	300	1.2	360
D	1000	3.33	3333
			6493 hours

Fig. 8.10. Order book

With a factory capacity of 5000 hours, then at least 1493 hours of work will have to be given out.

Figure 8.11 shows on what the decision about which garments are to be made outside is based.

Contrast the situation in Fig. 8.11 with the outcome (Fig. 8.12) had the

63

Style	Units Own	C.M.T.	S/R hrs per unit	Hrs req'd for own make	Contributions Per unit Own	C.M.T.	Own make	Given out
A	—	500	2		—	7	—	3 500
B	436	164	3	1 308	6	2	2 616	328
C	300	—	1.2	360	4	—	1 200	—
D	1 000	—	3.333	3 333	10	—	10 000	—
				5 001			13 816	3 828
TOTAL CONTRIBUTIONS							£17 644	

Fig. 8.11. Decision on garments to be made outside

Style	Apparent order of profitability on basis of c.p. hr	Units	Hours Per unit	Total	Contributions Per unit	Own make	C.M.T.
A	1	500 (Own)	2	1 000	8	4 000	
B	4	102 (Own)	3	306	6	612	
		498 (Cmt)		—	2		996
C	2	300 (Own)	1.2	360	4	1 200	
D	3	1 000 (Own)	3.33	3 333	10	10 000	
				4 999		15 812	996
TOTAL CONTRIBUTIONS						£16 808	

Fig. 8.12. Decision based on relative contribution per hour when garments made in own factory

decision been made purely on the basis of the relative contribution per hour when made in one's own factory.

It will readily be seen that, even in this modest example covering 5000 sewing room man hours of capacity, there could be a substantial improvement in contributions (and hence profit) by applying the techniques described in this chapter.

The use of the contribution concept for measuring the effect of capital expenditure

The evaluation of capital expenditure is greatly facilitated by knowledge of the fixed costs, the variable costs per unit, and the contribution, and by knowing which costs will alter in the changing situations.

The example in Fig. 8.13 demonstrates how clearly one can see the effect of changed situations.

Type of cost	Proposed method	Old method
Production (units) p.a.	12 000	8 000
Selling price	£3	£3
Total variable cost per unit	£0.70	£1
Contribution per unit	£2.30	£2
Contribution total	£27 600	£16 000
Capital cost of new machine	£10 000	
Incremental annual fixed cost associated with acquisition (depreciation, finance charges, space occupied, etc.)	£2 200	

Fig. 8.13. Comparative production data

1. Calculation of break-even quantity

$$= \frac{\text{Incremental fixed costs}}{\text{Unit contribution (diff. in variable unit costs)}}$$

$$= \frac{£2\,200}{0.30}$$

$$= 7\,333 \text{ units p.a.}$$

2. Calculation of return on investment

Incremental fixed capital   £10 000 (cost of machine, etc.)
Incremental variable capital £ 2 670 (extra inventory, debtors, etc.)

Increase in capital employed £12 670

$$\text{Rate of return} = \frac{\text{Incremental contribution} - \text{Increased fixed expenses}}{\text{Incremental capital employed}}$$

$$= \frac{(27\,600 - 16\,000) - 2200}{12\,670} \times 100$$

$$= \frac{9400 \times 100}{12\,670}$$

$$= 74.2\% \text{ (pre-tax)}$$

While initial calculations may show a handsome return on the increased capital employed, it would be an imprudent businessman who did not consider what the situation would be if certain of the basic presumptions were invalidated.

Let us consider Fig. 8.13 again and see what might result if, for a number of reasons, the projected targets were not reached.

1. Failure to sell more than 11 000 units.
2. Extra sales only achievable at 10 per cent mark down (discount).
3. Savings of variable costs only half of those expected.
4. Situation in which 1,2, and 3 all happen together.

Through knowledge of which costs are fixed and which are variable, and the use of this information, it is possible to measure the effects of failing to reach the expected targets of production, sales, and costs.

This is illustrated in Fig. 8.14.

	Old method	Proposed method	Failure to meet target			
			Failure to sell more than 11 000 units	Extra sales achieved only by 10% mark-down	Savings only half of expected	If all three happen
(a) Units sold p.a.	8 000	12 000	11 000	8 000 @ £3	12 000	8 000 @ £3
(b) Price	£3	£3	£3	4 000 @ £2.7	£3	3 000 @ £2.7
(c) Variable cost	£1	£0.70	£0.70	£0.70	£0.85	£0.85
(d) Fixed cost p.a.	£15 000	£17 200	£17 200	£17 200	£17 200	£17 200
Income p.a. (a) × (b)	£24 000	£36 000	£33 000	£34 800	£36 000	£32 100
Variable expenses (a) × (c)	8 000	8 400	7 700	8 400	10 200	9 350
Contribution	16 000	27 600	25 300	26 400	25 800	22 750
Fixed expenses (d)	15 000	17 200	17 200	17 200	17 200	17 200
PROFIT	£1 000	£10 400	£6 100	£9 200	£8 600	£5 550
Improvement		£9 400	£7 100	£8 200	£7 600	£4 550

Fig. 8.14. The risks of failure to meet targets

9

The contribution concept in other industries

Use of the contribution concept in a processing industry

So far, we have considered the use of the contribution concept in a labour-intensive industry. How does it adapt to a capital-intensive industry?

Again, it is a matter of identifying, first, the variable (or incremental) costs, and, second, the limiting resource that determines the optimum level of production.

Let us consider an example from the heavy chemical industry, concerned with the manufacture of starch-based products.

The products are used in a wide variety of industries, some of which are listed below:

Adhesives, pastes, etc.
Sizing for coating paper
Core gums for binding foundry sands
Envelope gums
Sizes for finishing textiles
Production of porous separators for electrical accumulators
Special starches for the food industry

The processes, which are all linked in a continuous plant, are shown in Fig. 9.1.

A further process of blending may be necessary if a small quantity with special characteristics is required.

In the making of pastes, further processing of mixing and packaging would be necessary.

Each of the products listed above can require different cooking times.

The basic role of labour is in machine-minding, handling input, and bagging off.

The limiting factor to production is the calcining process—the capacity of the huge pans for cooking.

The plant is run on a continuous 24 hour, 7 day week basis.

The process where the overwhelming proportion of the variable costs are incurred is in the provision of the heat necessary to convert the base starch into a calcined powder.

The mechanics of installing a pricing programme are the same as for the labour-intensive industry.

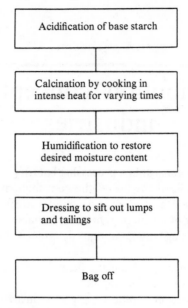

Fig. 9.1 Processes in manufacture of starch-based products

1. *Target for contributions for year*
This is calculated as follows:

Fixed expenses (per budget)	say	£200 000
Desired profit (% of capital employed)	say	£250 000
TARGET FOR CONTRIBUTIONS		£450 000

2. *Units of limiting factor*
We must be realistic about what effective plant hours we have for sale.

(a) Nominal capacity = 52 weeks × 168 hours	8736
(b) Reduce for holidays = 4 weeks × 168 hours	672
	8064
(c) Reduce for down-time (repairs not done in holidays, power cuts, strikes, etc.) say 10% =	806
SALEABLE PLANT HOURS	7258

3. *Target contribution per plant hour*
This follows easily from steps 1 and 2:

$$\frac{\text{Target contributions}}{\text{Saleable plant hours}} = \frac{£450\,000}{7258} = £62 \text{ per hour}$$

MAKING ORDER & COST/PRICE BUILD-UP								NO. 120/3	
Item	*Make*: 20 Tons (approx) core gum *Instructions*: 120cc HCL Cook 6 ton charges for 2 hours								
Line	*Category*	*Description*	*Lot no.*	*No. of bags*	*Bag wt (lbs)*	*Total wt (ton)*	*Price*	*Total*	*Per ton fin. prod.*
a		Maize	2412	200	140	12.5	170	2125.00	
b		Maize	2317	184	140	11.5	165	1897.50	
c		HCL						23.00	
d	Materials								
e									
f									
g				Input	a)	24.0		4045.50	
h		Loss factor: $\frac{a}{b}$	1.20	Output	b)	20.0			202.28
	Variable	*Process*	*Hr/ ton*	*V. cost p. hr*	*V. cost p. ton*	*Tons*			
i	cost of plant	Acidify ⎫							
j	operation	Calcine ⎪	0.40	30.0	12.0	20.0		240	12.00
k	(Gas, electricity,	Humidify ⎬							
l	labour, etc.)	Dress ⎭							
m	Other	Delivery charges							8.0
n	variable costs	Packing materials							15.0
o	(product-based)	etc.							
p	TOTAL VARIABLE COSTS (product-based)								237.28
q		Cash discount					$2\frac{1}{4}$%		
r	Variable costs	Sales commission					5%		
s	(price-based)								
t		TOTAL %					$7\frac{1}{4}$%		

Target selling price and contribution		
Variable cost (product-based) add Target contribution 0.4 Plant hrs × £62.0 c.p.h.		237.28 15.50
	$92\frac{1}{4}$%	252.78
Variable cost (price-based)	$7\frac{1}{4}$%	20.50
TARGET PRICE 100%		273.28

Actual selling price and contribution	
Selling price less Variable costs: Product-based (Line P) Price-based (Line T) $7\frac{1}{4}$% of S.P. = Contribution	260 −237.28 −19.50 = 3.22
Plants hours	0.4
CONTRIBUTION PER HOUR	£8.05

Fig. 9.2 Product cost build-up sheet

4. *Product cost build-up sheet*

The last step is to prepare a product cost build-up sheet (Fig. 9.2) for each type of product, showing the appropriate variable costs which are product-based:

Materials
Yield
Processing plant hours
Variable costs of operating plant
Packing and delivery

and also those variable costs which are price-based:

Sales commission

Cash discount

We are now in a position to build up the target selling price, and, conversely, calculate from the attainable selling price what the contribution per hour would be (see foot of Fig. 9.2).

When all the cost/price build-up sheets have been completed, the manufacturer is in a position to compare the relative value of each type of product to the company, as in Fig. 9.3.

Product		Core gum	Paper sizing	Textiles size	Adhesive	Speciality starch (food)
		£	£	£	£	£
Selling price	per ton	260	280	270	500	300
less Variable cost of subsequent processes (if any)	per ton	—	—	—	150	—
Net selling price (of main processing)	per ton	260	280	270	350	300
less Variable costs	per ton	256.68	250	260	240	240
= CONTRIBUTION	per ton	3.22	30	10	110	60
Plant hours per ton		0.4	0.5	0.4	0.3	0.3
= CONTRIBUTION PER PLANT HOUR		8.05	60.0	25.0	367	200

Fig. 9.3. Comparison of contribution of different products to overall profitability

It is clear that some products are more profitable than others. However, when the manager sees the comparisons so objectively, he can readily assess which products to concentrate on, which products need a price increase, and which products he could take a reduction on, if it meant getting a more than compensating volume of business which he could handle.

Although core gum shows up badly, a mere 5 per cent increase in selling price (from £260 to £273) would bring the contribution up to the target rate per hour.

Use of the contribution concept in retailing

So far, the use of the contribution concept has only been related to a manufacturing environment. Its usefulness in a retailing environment is now considered.

The objective is to help a retailer increase his profits by making the most advantageous use of the facilities available to him.

In pursuing this objective, it is necessary to:

1. Identify the facilities available and their extent.
2. Formulate an appropriate measure of the profits being made.
3. Relate the profits being made to the facilities available.

As profit is the reward of capital, the proper index of success should relate the results of trading to the facilities and resources used in the attainment of those results. Or, in financial terms, it should relate net profits to the capital employed in the business.

If profit planning is to be directed towards maximizing the net profit return on capital employed, it would be as well to start with an understanding of the nature of that capital employed.

Capital employed represents

Fixed assets (property, equipment, etc.)
  plus
Current assets (inventory, debtors, cash, etc.)
  less
Current liabilities (creditors for supplies, etc.)

To get a perspective on the employment of capital in the retail industry, it is interesting to look at the average percentages of capital employed shown in Fig. 9.4.

	Average of 12 major multiple and department stores	Average of 5 major mail-order companies
	%	%
Fixed assets	83.3	32.4
Current assets		
Inventory	23	30
Debtors	12.8	79
Other	9.1	10.2
Current liabilities	(28.2)	(51.6)
Capital employed	100	100

Fig. 9.4. Average of capital employed in retail industry

To calculate the return on capital employed at the end of a trading period is a purely historical exercise and does nothing to ensure the maximization of profits *during* the trading period.

What is needed, therefore, is some much more immediate index, which will influence the people actually doing the buying and selling throughout the trading period.

How, then, should we relate the goal of maximizing the return on capital employed to the day-to-day transactions?

Profits arise from the buying and selling of the various lines of merchandise. A proper index of profitability should therefore:

1. Identify the relative profitability of lines of merchandise.
2. Measure the extent to which each line of merchandise makes profitable use of whatever facilities are available.

The major items of capital employed in Fig. 9.4 were fixed assets and inventory.

71

Fixed assets represent the provision of store space and facilities in which goods are displayed and sold.

Inventory represents the investment in stocks of goods available for sale.

As capital employed is never limitless, in any retail establishment the twin constraints of money and space are invariably present. Any profit planning must be designed to achieve the greatest return within these constraints.

To assess objectively the relative economic benefits of selling various lines, it is necessary to consider four factors:

1. Percentage contribution (in the retailing industry called *margin*)
2. Sales turnover
3. Rate of stockturn (which, in turn, determines the amount of investment in inventory)
4. Selling space required

As will be seen, consideration of less than all four of the above can seriously mislead the retailer as to the true worth to the store of one line against another.

The factors are now considered progressively, stage by stage (with different apparent orders of profitability at each stage), until all four factors are considered in unison, giving a meaningful profit index for each line or department against another.

1. *Percentage margin* (*contribution*)

Too often, store management become obsessed with the single index of percentage margin, in many cases with scant attention to the level of turnover or rate of stockturn.

Unfortunately, the 'retail method' of inventory valuation, while it is convenient, encourages preoccupation with the average percentage margin for each department. This often leads to a universal mark-up in that department, and if certain goods cannot carry that mark-up then business is lost. Often to the detriment of overall business, the 'percentage margin' has become an end in itself, rather than a means to an end.

Such a superficial view could rate the separate lines as shown in Fig. 9.5.

Line	Percentage margin	Apparent order of profitability
A	38	2
B	32	3
C	30	4
D	40	1

Fig. 9.5. Percentage contribution (or 'margin')

2. *Sales turnover*

The percentage margin means little or nothing unless one knows the various volumes of £ sales to which the percentages must be applied.

72

It is the aggregate of margin £s that matters, for it is only when this aggregate exceeds the fixed costs of the store that any profit remains.

To see what contribution each line is making to the store's profits needs knowledge of the £ turnover done in each line, as shown in Fig. 9.6.

Line	Percentage margin	Turnover p.a. £	Contribution £	Apparent order of worth to the store
A	38	10 000	3 800	3
B	32	15 000	4 800	2
C	30	20 000	6 000	1
D	40	5 000	2 000	4

Fig. 9.6. Turnover and contribution

3. Stockturn

Because few stores have an unlimited supply of capital, it is necessary, before arriving at any conclusions as to the relative worth of any line to the store, to monitor the financial investment in stock needed to sustain the annual level of turnover in each line.

Does Line A represent the turnover of £1000 10 times per annum, or £2500 turning over 4 times a year, or something else?

Does Line B represent £5000 turning over 3 times a year, or £7500 turning over twice a year, or some other figure?

To take into account the investment involved therefore needs a knowledge of the annual rate of stockturn of each line. When this rate is applied, the apparent order of profitability is something quite different, as Fig. 9.7 shows.

Line (a)	Selling price (b) %	Margin on S.P. (c) %	Cost (investment) (d) = (b) − (c) %	Margin on investment (e) = (c) × 100 ÷ (d)	Stock-turns p.a. (f)	Gross margin on inv. p.a. (g) = (e) × (f) %	Apparent order of profitability
A	100	38	62	61.3	4	245.2	2
B	100	32	68	47.1	3.5	164.7	4
C	100	30	70	42.9	5	214.5	3
D	100	40	60	66.7	6	400.0	1

Fig. 9.7. Stockturn and apparent profitability

4. Selling space required

Figure 9.7 concerns itself only with that part of capital employed represented by investment in inventory (as low as 23 and 30 per cent in Table 9.4 on average capital employed). The implication of the index is that if one were in a position to concentrate sales on Line D, more and more profit would accrue, irrespective of its space requirements (which may be very extravagant).

For instance, if funds available for investment in inventory were limited to, say, £200 000, then the use of the gross margin on investment rule would, if applied to each of the four lines, show relative results as in Fig. 9.8.

Line	Funds for investment (a)	Stock-turns p.a. (b)	Permissible cost of sales (c) = (a) × (b)	Margin % on S.P. (d)	Margin £ (e) = (d) × (f)	Sales (f)	Apparent order of profitability
A	200 000	4	800 000	38	490 323	1 290 323	2
B	200 000	3.5	700 000	32	329 412	1 029 412	4
C	200 000	5	1 000 000	30	428 571	1 428 571	3
D	200 000	6	1 200 000	40	800 000	2 000 000	1

Note (f) is got by dividing (c) by the reciprocal of (d) i.e. 100% − 38% = 62%

Fig. 9.8. The use of gross margin on investment (ignoring space constraints)

The margins from Line D are considerably in excess of the other lines and would apparently yield by far the highest net profit.

But, if one were to recognize the other constraint, that of *space*, a different picture (Fig. 9.9) could emerge. Assume that the annual sales per square foot were as indicated in column (d) below, and that space was limited to 20 000 square feet.

Line (a)	Margins (b) £	Sales (c) £	Sales per sq. ft. (d) £	Space required (e) = (c) ÷ (d) sq. ft.	Space available (f) sq. ft.	Attainable margins (g) = (b) × (f) ÷ (e) sq. ft.	Revised profitability
A	490 323	1 290 323	52	24 814	20 000	395 199	2
B	329 412	1 029 412	42	24 510	20 000	268 798	4
C	428 571	1 428 571	70	20 408	20 000	420 000	1
D	800 000	2 000 000	36	55 556	20 000	288 000	3

Fig. 9.9. Space constraints and profitability

It will be seen that Line D, which appeared most profitable, because of its extravagant demand for space can no longer attain a margin of £800 000. As long as its sales performance is only £36 per square foot, then the maximum sales it could achieve in 20 000 square feet would be £720 000, which, at a margin of 40 per cent, would only yield a total margin of £288 000.

As long as there is a constraint of *space*, the use of any index which ignores its existence, and is based on margin alone, can prove seriously misleading.

Of the two constraints (money and space), the latter is likely to be the least flexible. Whereas surplus space is wasteful, surplus money can usually be found a profitable use.

Too little space is a long-term problem for correction, but money is constantly being added to by profits. It is often less difficult to find additional finance for a demonstrably profitable purpose than it is to find space.

Calculating a meaningful profit index
If now, in order to recognize this less flexible constraint of space, we were to

Line (a)	Annual sales per sq.ft. (b)	Margin % on sales (c)	Costs of goods (per sq.ft.)		Stockturns p.a. (f)	Investment per sq.ft. (g) = (e) ÷ (f)	Gross margin on investment % (h) = (b) × (c) ÷ (g)	Meaningful profit index (i) = (g) × (h)	Revised order of profitability
			% (d) = 100 − (c)	Amount (e) = (b) × (d)					
A	£52	38	62	£32.24	4	£8.06	245.2	19.76	2
B	42	32	68	28.56	3.5	8.16	164.7	13.44	4
C	70	30	70	49.00	5	9.8	214.5	21.00	1
D	36	40	60	21.6	6	3.6	400.0	14.4	3

Fig. 9.10. Calculation of meaningful profit index recognizing constraints of investment and space

apply the gross margin on investment to the investment per square foot, then a much more meaningful index of relative profitability would emerge.

It would give an index on which profit planning in pursuance of the desired goal of return on capital employed could properly be based, as the example in Fig. 9.10 shows.

It will be observed that the meaningful profit index represents the margin per square foot—i.e. (b) × (c)—a conception readily understood by all levels of store management.

It is the essential objective index of relative profitability for most stores.

It would be idle to pretend that, having calculated the index, one could drop all the less profitable lines and sell only the more profitable lines. Customers still expect a balanced range of merchandise. But when one can see the facts so objectively it helps the manager

1. To decide which lines are most profitable.
2. To decide which lines need a price lift.
3. To select a more profitable merchandise mix.
4. To think of how to achieve improvement (e.g., in space allocation, stockturns, prices, etc.).

The use of the margin per square foot index to motivate staff

In using the index of margin per square foot to motivate all grades of staff, it is first necessary to calculate what level of index one is aiming for.

This should be calculated by the following steps.

1. Budget the general operating expenses:
   Occupancy costs
   Administration costs
   Personnel costs
   Etc.
   Let us assume that these amount to £200 000 a year.
2. Decide what level of profit is desired—i.e., what return on capital employed is considered suitable. Let us assume that this amounts to 30 per cent per annum on £500 000 capital employed, giving a desired profit of £150 000.
3. Measure the floor space available. Let us assume that this amounts to 20 000 square feet.

To achieve profit goals requires a margin per square foot as follows:

(a) General operating expenses   £200 000
    Desired profit   150 000
    Total initial target margin   £350 000
(b) Square feet available   20 000
(c) Apportion the initial target margins over the selling departments, on a space basis.
(d) Add to the initial target margins for each department the direct labour and direct expenses of that department.

	Total	Dept. 1	Dept. 2	Dept. 3
General operating expenses	£200 000			
Desired profit	150 000			
Initial target margins	£350 000	£175 000	£122 500	£52 500
Space (sq. ft.)	20 000	10 000	7 000	3 000
Direct dept. labour and expenses	£43 000	£15 000	£17 500	£10 500
Total department target	£393 000	£190 000	£140 000	£63 000
Square feet		10 000	7 000	3 000
TARGET MARGIN PER SQ. FT.		£19	£20	£21

Fig. 9.11. Final total target margins

(e) This then gives the final total target margins for that department (see Fig. 9.11).

Each department manager now has a departmental target of margins for the year. He is aware of what average margin per square foot is needed to achieve that target.

It remains for him to know what margin per square foot each of his selling lines yields, so that he can set about improving his chances of achieving the target required.

When, for instance, the manager of the women's wear department knows the relative profitability of coats versus suits versus dresses versus knitwear, he can begin to plan where and how he is going to meet his target. If his reward is related to the achievement of his target, so much the better.

Within the women's wear department, he/she might be faced with the situation in Fig. 9.12.

	Sales per sq. ft.	Margin %	Apparent order of profitability on margin only	Margin per sq. ft.	New order of profitability
Coats	£49.7	34.9	5	£12.34	4
Suits	45.4	33.4	7	15.16	5
Rainwear	66.3	36.2	3	24.00	1
Dresses	33.6	35.7	4	12.00	8
Housefrocks	36.0	38.5	1	13.86	6
Furs	78.7	30.1	8	22.8	2
Skirts, slacks, and casualwear	39.9	34.5	6	13.77	7
Knitwear and blouses	48.4	36.7	2	17.62	3

Fig. 9.12. Comparison of profitability of various product lines, including space constraint

The above are actual figures obtained from store statistics. It should be observed that not one product group retained its superficial apparent order of profitability.

With this knowledge, how would the manager improve his performance?

77

The margin per square foot index is the product of price, cost, rate of stockturn, and space used.

The index can be influenced by changes in any one, or combination of more than one, of these factors. When one knows the relative index of one line against another, it becomes possible to experiment with engineering improvements in some of the lines.

Some stores are preoccupied with the maintenance of a departmental percentage margin, and because of this one often finds a percentage mark-up being applied inflexibly. Such inflexibility is tantamount to denying the existence of competition, and much store business is consequently being lost to other types of stores. This need not happen if stores would calculate their margin per square foot indices, and appraise alternative situations in terms of their yield of margins per square foot.

Consider dresses in Fig. 9.12, which have annual sales of £33.6 per square foot, margin of 35.7 per cent and stockturn of, say, 3.8 times a year. Column 2 in Fig. 9.13 shows the effect of a 5 per cent price reduction and increase in rate of stockturn to 6 times a year. Column 3 shows what might be achieved by improved use of space. Column 4 assumes both of these changes happen.

	Originally	Assume 5% drop in S.P. and stockturn up to 6 p.a.	Assume better use of space	Assume both were possible
(a) Selling price	£50	£47.50	£50	£47.50
(b) Margin	35.7%	32.3%	35.7%	32.3%
(c) Margin £	£17.85	£15.35	£17.85	£15.35
(d) Cost (a) − (c)	£32.15	£32.15	£32.15	£32.15
(e) Stockturns p.a.	3.8	6.0	3.8	6.0
(f) Sales p.a. (a) × (e)	£190	£285	£190	£285
(g) Margins p.a. (f) × (b)	£67.83	£92	£67.83	£92
(h) Sales per sq. ft.	£33.6	£44.2	£38	£57
(i) Space occupied (f) ÷ (h)	5.65	5.65	5.00	5.0
(j) Margin per sq. ft. (g) ÷ (i)	£12.00	£16.29	£13.57	£18.40

Fig. 9.13. Effect of changes in price, stockturn, and better use of space on a product's profitability

When the manager is aware of his target and is fed with objective information, he is better equipped to pursue the desired return on capital employed.

The object of the exercise is to increase the total amount of margins within the constraints of the limits of finance and space.

Maximum profit arises from the highest aggregate of margins out of which to meet the fixed expenses of the business, with the maximum net profit remaining.

Use of the contribution concept in a multi-product multi-factory situation

It is not uncommon in industry to find a parent company with several subsidiary companies, or a single company with several factories, making a wide range of broadly similar products, the manufacture of which can be switched from one factory to another as management deems opportune.

Take, for instance, a clothing group whose product ranges from light clothing—such as blouses, childrens' wear, etc., through anoraks, skirts, slacks, etc.—to the heavier clothing, such as tailored suits and topcoats.

It is probable that the heavier clothing, which may demand more specialized machinery and a greater division and training of labour, may be concentrated in one or two factories. On the other hand, the lighter, simpler clothing may use more standard less specialized machinery and be capable of a greater degree of transferability from one factory to another, as circumstances may suggest.

The problem is that the various factories may have:

Different overhead costs
Different allowed making times
Different operator performances
Different rates of pay
Different facilities and capital employed
Different arbitrary methods of apportioning overheads.
Carry an arbitrary apportionment of group head office costs

Yet it is desired that the group should have a common, and rational, pricing structure, which at the same time will facilitate the maximization of profits.

To achieve this objective, it is necessary to know

The variable cost of each product made in each factory, and the resultant contribution
The standard hours produced in each factory
The overhead costs in total
The capital employed in each product group
The desired rate of return on capital employed

From this information it will be possible to ascertain:

The target for contributions
The effective hours over which the contributions need to be recovered
The target selling price
The relative advantages of different locations for making certain products

1. Target for contributions

Simply stated, this is the aggregate overhead expenses plus the desired profit. The latter is usually calculated as a return on capital employed.

It is not unreasonable, with a wide product range, to want prices to reflect the differing amounts of capital employed in producing the various products. Also, if this were not so, the less capital-intensive products would be subsidizing the more capital-intensive products, and this might result in prices that jeopardized the group's competitive position for the former products.

For the purpose of differentiating between the amounts of capital employed by each product group, it may only be necessary to classify the range into three divisions—light clothing, medium clothing, and heavy clothing.

Thereafter, it is a matter of examining each item of capital employed and analysing it as appropriately as possible—as in Fig. 9.14, for example.

Item of capital employed	Comment	Total	Light	Medium	Heavy
Land and buildings	This may be a mixture of rented and freehold property, allocated rather arbitrarily between the three groups. It would probably be fairer to allocate the property among the groups on the basis of nominal capacity.				
Machinery	This should be analysed on as factual an allocation as possible.				
Stocks: cloth, etc work-in-process finished garments	It is not likely to be difficult to allocate these accurately.				
Debtors	The customers for each type of clothing and the amount outstanding from each customer are probably known, so it should be fairly simple to make an accurate estimate of the capital tied up in debtors for each group.				
(Creditors)	This negative figure can be allocated on the basis of the cloth, etc., purchased in each of the three product groups.				

Fig. 9.14. Analysis of capital employed

After identifying the capital employed in each product group, the next step is to decide what rate of return is needed on that capital to

Combat inflation
Reward shareholders
Finance growth

When the desired rate of return has been decided, and the profit required from each group calculated, it is then necessary to evaluate the sales of each group of clothing into standard machining hours.

Dividing the desired profit for each group by the standard machining hour content of their respective sales gives a contribution per machining hour needed to cover the desired profit, or return on capital employed, for that group.

To this must be added a contribution rate per machining hour to cover the overheads (which is done by dividing the aggregate overheads by the aggregate effective machining hours available, as calculated in 2 below), and the result is a composite contribution rate per machining hour for each group, to apply to the variable costs in order to arrive at target selling prices.

2. Effective hours available

From the target for contributions follows the amount over and above the variable costs that has to be recovered, over the saleable production made, in order to meet profit objectives.

In pursuing this aim, it should be recognized that there is a limit to the number of garments that each factory can produce. In a clothing factory, this limit is almost invariably set by the number of effective machining (or sewing) hours available.

Why machining hours? If we examine the other processes we find that they have more flexibility. The output of the cutting process can vary considerably if the height (or number) of lays that are cut together, is altered.

When under pressure, the examining process can be skimped or done by sampling.

The pressing process can be done less thoroughly.

The packing process can depend on the size of the order (whether packed singly or in dozens) and the method of despatch (whether boxed or hanging on rails).

But machining is done singly and *must* be complete.

To use the total direct labour (rather than just machining) could distort performance statistics and invalidate the calculation of hours of limiting factor over which the contributions are to be applied.

To recover the target contributions over the effective machining hours

Factory	A	B	C	D
Nominal capacity				
No. of employees	100	150	80	200
x hours p.a.	2 080	2 080	2 080	2 080
	208 000	312 000	166 400	416 000
Reduce for holidays				
25 days × 8 hours, i.e., 200 hours per employee	20 000	30 000	16 000	40 000
	188 000	282 000	150 400	376 000
Reduce for absenteeism %	15	17	12	16.5
Attended hours, therefore,	159 800	234 060	132 952	313 960
Apply average % utilization	80	82	90	85
Utilized hours	102 272	175 545	119 117	240 178
Apply average % performance	80	75	100	90
= EFFECTIVE MACHINING HOURS PRODUCED	102 272	175 545	119 117	240 178
There are, respectively, of the nominal capacity hours (%)	44.2	56	71.5	57.7

Fig. 9.15. Calculation of effective machining hours available

available means being realistic about what standard hour content of saleable goods is being produced—i.e., the effective hours of the limiting factor.

So the calculation shown in Fig. 9.15 should be made for each factory in the group.

Unless and until any action is taken to improve this situation, these are the effective machining hours over which the profit target has to be met.

The outcome of stages 1 and 2 is:

Amount of return on capital employed (in each production group)	$\div$	Standard machining hour content of products in groups	$=$	Recovery rate per standard machining hour
Add Overheads	$\div$	Effective machining hours	$=$	Recovery rate per standard machining hour

$$= \text{COMPOSITE RATE PER STANDARD HOUR TO RECOVER}$$
$$\text{TARGET CONTRIBUTIONS FOR EACH PRODUCT GROUP}$$

3. *Target selling price*

A target selling price would then be built up as shown in Fig. 9.16.

Materials	× × ×
Direct labour (rather than machining)	× × ×
Machining: Hours ×	
Rate ×	
Cost × ×	× ×
VARIABLE COST	× × ×
Contributions: Machining hrs × contribution per hour	× ×
TARGET SELLING PRICE	× × ×

Fig. 9.16. Calculation of target selling price

4. *Relative advantages of different locations for making certain products*

The next step is to work out how to maximize profits, bearing in mind the possibility of making certain products in different factories.

To illustrate the use of the contribution concept in this exercise, four different products are considered, each of which is capable of being made at any of four different factories.

It is first necessary to know what comparable contribution each product would yield when made in each of the four factories.

The products are W, X, Y, and Z, and each is made in factories A, B, C, and D. Figure 9.17 gives the data for each product at the factories.

Factory	A	B	C	D
Product W				
Materials	2.00	2.00	2.00	2.00
Direct labour				
(other than machining)	0.20	0.20	0.20	0.20
Machining: Hrs	1.00	1.25	0.80	1.30
Rate	1.00	0.95	1.20	1.00
Cost	1.00	1.19	0.96	1.30
VARIABLE COST	3.20	3.39	3.16	3.50
SELLING PRICE	5.20	5.20	5.20	5.20
CONTRIBUTION	2.00	1.81	2.04	1.70
(S.P. − V.C.)				
CONTRIBUTION PER				
MACHINING HOUR	2.00	1.45	2.55	1.31
Product X				
Materials	3.00	3.00	3.00	3.00
Direct labour				
(other than machining)	0.15	0.15	0.15	0.15
Machining: Hrs	0.50	0.80	0.40	0.70
Rate	1.00	0.95	1.20	1.20
Cost	0.50	0.76	0.48	0.70
VARIABLE COST	3.65	3.91	3.63	3.85
SELLING PRICE	5.15	5.15	5.15	5.15
CONTRIBUTION	1.50	1.24	1.52	1.30
(S.P. − V.C.)				
CONTRIBUTION PER				
MACHINING HOUR	3.00	1.55	3.80	1.86
Product Y				
Materials	1.75	1.75	1.75	1.75
Direct labour				
(other than machining)	0.10	0.10	0.10	0.10
Machining: Hrs	0.75	0.50	0.60	0.75
Rate	1.00	0.95	1.20	1.00
Cost	0.75	0.475	0.72	0.75
VARIABLE COST	2.60	2.325	2.57	2.60
SELLING PRICE	4.10	4.10	4.10	4.10
CONTRIBUTION				
(S.P. − V.C.)	1.50	1.775	1.53	1.50
CONTRIBUTION PER				
MACHINING HOUR	2.00	3.55	2.55	2.00

Fig. 9.17. (*continued over*)

(*continued from p.* 83)

Factory	A	B	C	D
Product Z				
Materials	1.80	1.80	1.80	1.80
Direct labour				
(other than machining)	0.10	0.10	0.10	0.10
Machining: Hrs	0.25	0.333	0.20	0.225
Rate	1.00	0.95	1.20	1.00
Cost	0.25	0.317	0.24	0.225
VARIABLE COST	2.15	2.217	2.14	2.125
SELLING PRICE	3.60	3.60	3.60	3.60
CONTRIBUTION				
(S.P. – V.C.)	1.45	1.383	1.46	1.475
CONTRIBUTION PER				
MACHINING HOUR	5.80	4.15	7.30	6.55

Fig. 9.17. Calculation of comparable contributions in each factory

Factory	A	B	C	D
Effective machining hours available	102 272	175 545	119 117	140 178
Product				
W Quantity	300 000	300 000	300 000	300 000
Hrs per unit	1.0	1.25	0.8	1.3
Contribution per hour	£2.00	£1.45	£2.55	£1.31
Hours	300 000	375 000	240 000	390 000
Contributions	£600 000	£543 750	£612 000	£510 900
X Quantity	150 000	150 000	150 000	150 000
Hrs per unit	0.5	0.8	0.4	0.7
Contribution per hour	£3.0	£1.55	£3.80	£1.86
Hours	75 000	120 000	60 000	105 000
Contributions	£225 000	£186 000	£228 000	£195 300
Y Quantity	200 000	200 000	200 000	200 000
Hrs per unit	0.75	0.5	0.6	0.75
Contribution per hour	£2.00	£3.55	£2.55	£2.00
Hours	150 000	100 000	120 000	150 000
Contributions	£300 000	£355 000	£306 000	£300 000
Z Quantity	400 000	400 000	400 000	400 000
Hrs per unit	0.25	0.333	0.20	0.225
Contribution per hour	£5.80	£4.15	£7.30	£6.55
Hours	100 000	133 333	80 000	90 000
Contributions	£580 000	£553 332	£584 000	£589 500

Fig. 9.18. Contributions of W, X, Y, and Z

Assume that sales are as follows:

300 000 units of Product W
150 000 units of Product X
200 000 units of Product Y
400 000 units of Product Z

We can evaluate what these would mean in terms of comparable machining hours required and contribution yields in each factory, as shown in Fig. 9.18.

If it were a matter of placing sales to the factories where they would yield the highest contribution per machining hour, then Product W would go to Factory C; Product X would go to Factory C; Product Y would go to Factory B; and Product Z would go to factory C.

But, as Fig. 9.19 shows, this would produce a gross imbalance of hours of production against hours available.

Factory	Product	Desired loading	Hours available
A	—	Nil	102 272
B	Y	100 000	175 545
C	W	240 000	
	X	60 000	
	Z	80 000	
		380 000	119 117
D	—	—	240 178

Fig. 9.19. Machine hours available and desired loading for W, X, Y, and Z

This is clearly a totally impractical and unacceptable situation.

If next it were attempted to load the factories on a one-product one-factory basis, in line with each factory's availability of hours, then production might be arranged as in Fig. 9.20.

Factory A	with a capacity of 102 272 hours would probably get the 400 000 units of Product Z, utilizing 100 000 hours and yielding contributions of	£580 000
Factory C	with a capacity of 119 117 hours would probably get the 200 000 units of Product Y, utilizing 120 000 hours and yielding contributions of	£306 000
Product D	with a capacity of 240 178 hours would probably get the 150 000 units of Product X (because it has a better contribution than the remaining Factory B), utilizing 105 000 hours and yielding contributions of	£195 300
	The remaining 135 178 hours would be taken up with 104 000 units of Product W, yielding contributions of	£177 083
Factory B	with a capacity of 175 545 hours would be taken up with 140 436 units of Product W, yielding contributions of	£254 540
TOTAL CONTRIBUTIONS		£1 512 923

Fig. 9.20. Production arranged on a one-product one-factory basis

85

This would still leave the sales of Product W undercovered:

Sales   300 000 units

Production: Factory D 104 000

           Factory B 104 036

                        244 036 units

          Shortage   55 964 units

However, if the factories are loaded, within their hours available, first with the product on which they have the greatest contribution advantage over the other factories, then production would be arranged as follows.

Product Y if made in Factory B has a £49 000 advantage over the next highest, and B is therefore given the 200 000 units of Y, which will occupy 100 000 hours and yield £355 000 of contribution.

Product W if made in Factory C has a £12 000 greater yield than if made in the next best (i.e., A). To the extent of the 119 117 hours available in Factory C, 148 896 units of Product W will be made there yielding £303 748 of contributions. The remaining 102 272 units of Product W will be made in A, the next best, representing 102 272 hours of production and yielding £204 544 of contribution.

Product Z if made in Factory D will have a £5500 greater contribution yield than if made in C, which is now full, and £9500 greater contribution yield than if made in Factory A. Product Z will therefore be made in Factory D, using 90 000 hours and yielding £589 500 of contribution.

Of the remaining products (i.e., 150 000 units of Product X, and 60 436 units of Product W), because the contribution on X is better in Factory D than in Factory B, the 150 000 units of X should be allocated to Factory D. Because the contribution on Product W is better in Factory B than in Factory D, they should be allocated to Factory B.

The resultant factory loading and predicted contributions would be as shown in Fig. 9.21.

This yields an increase in contributions, and hence profits of (£1 757 632 minus £1 512 923) £245 000, and still leaves capacity available in Factory D of 45 718 machining hours.

Factory	Capacity	Product	Units	Hours	Contribution £
A	102 272 hrs	W	102 272	102 272	204 544
B	175 545	Y	200 000	100 000	355 000
		W	60 436	75 545	109 540
C	119 117	W	148 896	119 117	303 748
D	240 178	X	150 000	105 000	195 300
		Z	400 000	90 000	589 500
TOTAL CONTRIBUTIONS					1 757 632

Fig. 9.21. Optimum arrangement of production of W, X, Y, and Z

In the foregoing example, which covers only four products and four factories, the optimization of contributions and the allocation of products to factories have been done by observation and deduction. In the case of many products and numerous factories, such an exercise could well use the assistance of a computer.

The factory loading arrived at should not stand for all time. Efficiencies, utilization, attendance, contributions, and prices have a habit of improving once they are seen to be measured objectively. The changing situation should be monitored regularly, so that management decisions can be made on updated information.

10

Special problems

The treatment of quantity discounts

The case for a quantity discount or reduction in selling price, usually put forward by a customer who places orders for large volumes, is argued as follows:

1. Large volumes permit the manufacturer to buy his raw materials more economically.
2. Large quantities make possible the more efficient use of labour, longer runs, fewer changes in style, and better flow of work.
3. It makes possible a more efficient use of materials.
4. Packaging in bulk, rather than in small lots, is possible.
5. Selling charges are smaller, because of bulk deliveries.
6. Selling costs are lower.
7. There are fewer demands on administration, documentation, credit control, etc.

Some of these reasons are perfectly valid, but some are not. For instance, does having a big customer lead, because of a reduced number of orders, to saving the cost of a part or the whole of a salesman? Often big customers command the attention of the more highly paid chief executive, and with this goes more expensive hospitality, with the salesman in attendance to handle the details of the order.

Many of the apparent advantages depend on the total volume representing long runs of few styles, rather than shorter runs of a greater variety of styles.

Are the goods to be delivered to a central store, or are they to be distributed far and wide, to a large number of retail outlets in the customer's group?

When it is clear what the *nature* of the discount-seeking volume is, the product should be re-costed and as close an estimate as possible made of the economies which may be realized.

Thus calculation of the quantity discount for the two-piece suit in the example on page 44 might look like Fig. 10.1.

The quantity price is 88.8 per cent of the normal price build-up, which indicates that, for quantities that would enable the assumed economies to be made, a quantity discount of 10 per cent off the normal price could be offered.

If, as is likely, more than one product is involved, then a range of re-costings should be undertaken. It is possible that the customer would only be interested in one rate of quantity discount, not different rates for various products.

	Normal production (£ cost per unit)	Saving	Quantity production (£ cost per unit)
Piece goods	6.50	10% saving on volume purchase from mills	5.85
Lining & trimmings	1.75	10% saving, as above	1.575
Labour			
Cutting	0.605	50%, due to cutting greater no. of plies	0.30
Sewing (5 hrs)	2.52	5% due to fewer (4.75 hrs) variety changes	2.395
Finishing	0.55	Nil	0.55
Packing	0.25	40% due to bulk packing	0.15
Delivery	0.15	66% due to bulk deliveries	0.05
VARIABLE COSTS (product-based)	12.325	VARIABLE COSTS (product-based)	10.87
Contribution 5 hr × £1.85	9.25	4.75 hr × £1.85	8.788
(92%)	21.575	(94½%)	19.658
Cash discount 3%		Same	
Commission 5%		Reduced to 2½%	
TARGET SELLING PRICE (100%)	£23.429	TARGET SELLING PRICE (100%)	£20.80

Fig. 10.1. Costs and selling price for normal and quantity production

Therefore, to assess what that single rate should be, a representative selection of calculated discounts over the range of products involved should be made.

The above examples were calculated on a target selling price basis. It might be wondered what happens where the actual selling price is at the market price, which is below the target selling price. In these circumstances, a manufacturer should aim for the same rate of contribution per hour from the quantity production price as he expects from the normal production price.

For example, if the actual selling (market) price in Fig. 10.1 were £22.00 per unit, the contribution would be as shown in Fig. 10.2.

	Normal production price
Actual selling price	£22.00
less Cash discounts 3%	£0.66
Commission	£1.10
	£20.24
less Variable costs (product-based)	£12.325
= Contribution	£7.915
÷ Sewing time	5 hr
= CONTRIBUTION PER HOUR	£1.583

Fig. 10.2. Normal production and contribution per hour

	Quantity production price £
Variable costs (product-based)	10.87
+ Contribution 4.75 hr × £1.583 cph	7.52
(94½%)	18.39
+ Contribution 3% on S.P.	0.58
+ Commission 2½% on S.P.	0.49
SELLING PRICE (100%)	19.46

Fig. 10.3. Quantity production and contribution per hour

If we now build up the quantity production price, it would be as shown in Fig. 10.3.

The resultant quantity price of £19.46 is 88.45 per cent of the actual selling price of normal production. This would indicate that the previously calculated quantity discount of 10 per cent off normal production selling price is still applicable.

Transfer pricing

A transfer price can be defined as 'the price at which the product of one member firm of a group is transferred (or sold) to another member of the group'.

Where such products are of significant volume, management has considerable scope, if it is so minded, to manipulate the profits as between member firms of a group. For example, by arranging a low transfer price, the profits of the supplying company can be depressed and those of the recipient company increased.

This kind of profit manipulation, if it is not regulated, can reduce the aggregate tax liability of a group of companies. It can also reduce the cost to the companies of paying those who are remunerated by a share of profits, commission based on profits, or a scheme of distribution of profits above a target level.

There is little to be gained by profit manipulation for tax-saving purposes if the entire group is within one country. The possibility of making subvention payments within the group, to offset a subsidiary company's losses, makes profit manipulation in such cases unnecessary. However, when the group is multi-national, profit manipulation by transfer pricing can move profits from high-tax countries to lower-tax countries. Tax authorities are very conscious of such possibilities and tend to be suspicious of this kind of transfer pricing.

If profit-sharing is to be used as a means of motivating company executives and workers, the company's profits must be fairly calculated. Suspicion that profits were being manipulated by rigging transfer prices would destroy an incentive very quickly.

For these reasons, therefore, a transfer price must be an equitable price. To give confidence to parties interested, the bases on which such prices are computed must be consistent. Of all the prices that a company fixes, the ones most open to question—sometimes long after the event—are its transfer prices. It follows, therefore, that it is wise to record at the time the rules according to which such prices were arranged.

Situations vary, and there may be legitimate and sound business reasons for arranging lower than normal prices for some inter-group transactions. Here is an example.

It may be that one member company is short of work, and also has excessive stocks of raw materials.

Frequently it is more profitable to make up raw materials for another member company to sell as finished products at discounted prices, rather than sell the raw materials.

This has the advantage of keeping the work force intact and busy, at the same time reducing raw material stocks that might otherwise be difficult to move as such.

The transfer price in such circumstances might legitimately be lower than a normal transfer price. However, as it may have to be justified later, it is important to record the circumstances at the time. Where executives are remunerated in part by profit-sharing, it could also be sensible to advise them and record their acquiesence.

The use of market prices as an indication of what a transfer price should be is seldom helpful because inter-firm transfers of goods may take place at different stages of manufacture.

In using the contribution concept for transfer pricing four main options are available.

1. Transfer at *variable cost* only.
2. Transfer at *break-even cost*—i.e., variable cost plus contribution rate which would recoup the fixed costs.
3. Transfer at *full price*—i.e., variable cost plus a contribution rate which would recoup both fixed and target profit.
4. Transfer at a *price which would share the profit between the supplier company and the receiving company.*

Because inter-group transfers of goods are often in bulk, differently packed and transported from normal production, there should be a separate cost build-up reflecting the facts of the situation.

To illustrate the four options above, let us consider how a gent's two-piece suit, similar to the one on page 44, might have been priced for inter-group transfer.

The normal cost build-up of this item is shown in Fig. 10.4.

Materials
Piece goods	6.50	
Linings and trimmings	1.75	
		8.25

Direct labour
Cutting	0.605	
Sewing	2.52	
Finishing	0.55	
		3.675

Other variable costs (product-based)
Delivery charges	0.25	
Packing materials	0.15	
		0.40

TOTAL VARIABLE COSTS (product-based)   12.325

There were, in addition, variable costs which were price-based of

Cash discount	3%
Sales commission	5%
Total	8%

The target selling price for normal sales was built up thus:

Variable cost (product based) add Target contribution	£12.325
5 sewing hours × £1.85 per hr	9.25
	21.575 = 92% of selling price
Variable cost (price based) 8%	1.874 = 8%
TARGET SELLING PRICE	£23.439 = 100%

Fig. 10.4. Normal cost build-up for gent's two-piece suit

Before the four options are illustrated, let us recap on how the target contribution rate per hour was calculated.

The formula was:

	Amount £	÷	*Saleable hrs*	=	*Target cont. rate per hour*
Fixed expenses (per budget) say	70.150		48.730		1.44
+					
Desired profit	20.000				0.41
TARGET CONTRIBUTIONS	90.150				1.85

The options can now be illustrated in Fig. 10.5.

If, in the case of inter-group transfers, there are no price-based variable costs (like cash discount or sales commission), these prices would be the basic transfer prices.

	1. Variable Costs only	2. Variable cost plus cont. rate to cover fixed exps.	3. Variable cost plus cont. rate to cover fixed exps. and target profit	4. Variable cost plus cont. rate to cover fixed exps. and part of target profit
	£	£	£	£
Materials	8.25	8.25	8.25	8.25
Direct labour	3.675	3.675	3.675	3.675
Other variable exps. (product-based)	0.40	0.40	0.40	0.40
VARIABLE COSTS (product-based)	12.325	12.325	12.325	12.325
Contribution (Opt. 2) 5 hrs × 1.44 (Opt. 3) 5 hrs × 1.85 (Opt. 4) see Fig. 10.6		7.2	9.25	8.36
TRANSFER PRICE	12.325	19.525	21.575	20.685

Fig. 10.5. Options for transfer pricing

Option 1. This represents the very minimum a transfer price should be. It does little other than recover the out-of-pocket costs and its only merit is that it keeps the labour force together and occupied at a normal working tempo.

Option 2. This recovers out-of-pocket costs and makes a contribution to fixed costs.

Option 3. This is the ideal choice for the supplying company, but would probably mean that the receiving company could not itself make a profit on the product's ultimate sale.

Option 4. This is the most likely choice. The one decision left is how to share the profit between the two parties to the transfer. Such a division can be an arbitrary split, or one based on added value or conversion costs. Bearing in mind the need for apparent fairness in transfer pricing, the arbitrary split may not be acceptable, and therefore a more 'logical' split is desirable.

The example in Fig. 10.6 is based on sharing the profit element in proportion to each party's added value or conversion costs.

The only area of likely dispute is in assessing each party's chargeable fixed costs. It is often the case that, in arranging inter-group transfer prices, authority rests with, or reference is made to, a central group executive. He may make the final allocation if necessary.

The parties to the transfers may be companies of different size, with very different scales of fixed costs. It could be that, in deciding which fixed costs are appropriate, the arbitrator will decide to use the contribution rates per hour of the supplier company, the one with the major interest in the transaction.

Assume, then, that this is the case, and that the contribution rate per hour for fixed costs of £1.44 could be further subdivided into 0.24 p per hour for fixed selling costs and £1.20 for all other fixed costs. We can now proceed to calculate a transfer price, as Fig. 10.6 shows.

	Company A (supplier) £	Company B (receiver) £	Total £
Assumed ultimate selling price		25.00	25.00
After transfer costs			
Cash discount 3%		0.75	
Sales commission 5%		1.25	
Delivery to customer		0.30	
Fixed selling costs			
(5 hrs × 0.24p)		1.20	
		3.50	3.50
Divided profit (see below)	2.36	0.815	
Pre-transfer conversion costs			
Direct labour	3.675		
Delivery & packing to B	0.40		
A's fixed costs (excl. selling)			
(5 hr × £1.20 p hr)	6.00		
	10.075		10.075
Materials	8.25		8.25
TRANSFER PRICE	20.685	20.685	
		Profit	3.175

Fig. 10.6. Calculation of transfer price

Profit of £3.175 is divisible between A and B in proportion to their conversion costs—i.e., A £10.075, and B £3.50.

Example

$$A = £3.175 \times 10.075 \div 13.575 = £2.36$$
$$B = £3.175 \times 3.50 \div 13.575 = 0.815$$
$$£3.175$$

Variations on this approach can include:

1. The treatment of cash discount as a reduction of selling price rather than a Company B cost.
2. Ignoring the fixed expenses and sharing the contribution which remains after deducting both parties' costs from the selling price on the basis of each party's conversion costs.

If we assume that both these variations are applied, the calculation of the transfer price between Company A and Company B would appear as in Fig. 10.7.

	Company A (supplier) £	Company B (seller) £	Total £
Selling price		25.00	25.00
less Cash discount (3%)		0.75	0.75
= Net selling price		24.25	24.25
After transfer costs			
Sales commission 5%		1.25	
Delivery to customer		0.30	
		1.55	1.55
Pre-transfer conversion costs			
Direct labour	3.675		
Delivery and packing	0.400		
	4.075		4.075
Materials	8.250		8.250
Contribution	7.516	2.859	10.375
TRANSFER PRICE	19.841	19.841	—

Fig. 10.7. **Variations in calculating transfer price**

Whichever method is used, it has to have enough logical basis to satisfy the interested parties that it is reasonably fair. Once it has been accepted, to avoid creating suspicion its use should be consistent. Any variations from the chosen method, for special occasions, should be adequately documented. They may have to be justified at a later date.

Of course, as far as the supplier company is concerned, the more goods he

	Total	Assume 20% of saleable hrs at transfer price work	Normal work
(a) Saleable hours	48 730 hrs —	9 746 =	38 984
(b) Fixed expenses	£70 150 (or £1.40 p hr)	£11 695 — (at £1.20 p hr) =	£58 455
(c) Target profit	£20 000 (or £0.41 p hr)	3 733 — (at 0.383 p hr) =	£16 267
(d) Target contributions (b) + (c)	£90 150	£15 428	£74 722
(e) Target contribution per hour (d) ÷ (a)	£1.85	£1.58 New target	£1.92

Fig. 10.8. **Effect on target profit of transfer price work**

95

transfers at less than his full target selling price, the more he will have to load his other business to meet his target profit.

The example in Fig. 10.8 assumes that 20 per cent of his production capacity is engaged on inter-group transfer price work, and shows how the contribution rate on the remaining work would have to be raised to meet target profits.

The aggregate of all contributions must be enough to meet the fixed expenses and desired profit. What the company fails to make on some items, it must make up on the others. This is why it is important to maintain the contribution progress record discussed earlier, and illustrated in Fig. 7.9.

11

Conclusion

Examples have been given of how to relate contributions to the limiting factor in a labour-intensive industry, a capital-intensive industry, and the retail industry.

In each of these cases profit could receive a considerable boost as a result of the discipline of using 'the contribution per unit of limiting factor' concept to decide which products are economically most beneficial to the company. Getting this increased profit does not have to involve raising prices—just knowing which products make the most profitable use of the facilities available.

In addition, a more logical method of building up selling prices is provided, undistorted by arbitrary allocations of overhead expanses.

A reliable indication is possible, while selling is in progress, of the extent to which targets for profitability and utilization of capacity are being achieved.

The use of the methods recommended in this book also make possible control by means of a weekly profit and loss statement (Fig. 46) which can be further refined by the application of variances from standard cost and/or budgeted overheads.

Appendix. The pricing/profit management exercise

You are reading your morning paper at breakfast and note, while drinking your coffee that:

The miners have just got a large pay rise.
The balance of payments still doesn't.
The chairman of Sparks and Mencers, while still making noises about high costs, is still increasing his turnover.

You have appointments today with your three customers, who you expect will place their orders for the coming period.

You have your own problems: rising costs, and the need to keep the factory full of work and, at the same time, produce results which will keep the bank and the shareholders reasonably happy.

The information available to you is set out in Fig. A.1.

Last year's sales
Total
Product A: 50 000 units at average S.P. of £6.666
Product B: 50 000 units at average S.P. of £3.333

- -

Sparks and Mencers
A: 20 000 units @ £6.75
B: 30 000 units @ £3.25

Nat Stores
A: 15 000 units @ £6.72
B: 10 000 units @ £3.40

Smallwoods
A: 15 000 units @ £6.50
B: 10 000 units @ £3.50

- -

Last year's results

Sales turnover	£500 000
Materials	250 000
Labour	100 000
Overheads	100 000
PROFIT	£50 000
Capital employed	£200 000
Number of direct labour employees	100
Direct labour hours available per annum	200 000

Fig. A.1. Information for pricing/profit management exercise

You make two products: A and B.

Last year A had £3 worth of material content, and its standard making time is three hours.

B had £2 worth of material content, and its standard making time is one hour.

Materials are expected to rise this year by 25 per cent.

Labour rates are expected to rise this year by 20 per cent.

Overheads are expected to rise this year by 15 per cent.

The buyer from each of your three customers will be calling on you to learn your prices and (you hope) place his orders.

Your basic product cost information is set out in Fig. A.2.

```
Cost: Product A
Materials £3 + 25%        = £3.75
Labour 3 hr × 50p + 20% = £1.80
Overheads
Profits
SELLING PRICE     _____
```

```
Cost: Product B
Materials £2 + 25%        = £2.50
Labour 1 hr × 50p + 20% =    60
Overheads
Profit
SELLING PRICE     _____
```

Fig. A.2. Costs for Products A and B

The sellers were 'given' the variable costs of materials and labour, and what was required of them was to fix their selling prices and policy.

The customers' buyers were briefed as follows:

1. It was their policy not to be dependent on a single supplier.
2. In total, from their various suppliers, they should try to increase their orders by 10 per cent.
3. Because of their knowledge of each other's mark-ups and selling prices, they could calculate the average price they each paid for Product A and Product B.
4. They were to visit each 'manufacturer' and negotiate volumes and prices, and place whatever orders they deemed advisable.

Examples of the variety of profit levels resulting from this exercise are shown in Figs. A.3–5.

Sales

Product A

Sparks & Mencers	21 000	units @ £7.35 = 154 350
Nat Stores	20 000	units @ £7.05 = 141 000
Smallwoods	20 000	units @ £7.10 = 142 000
Total	61 000	

Product B

Sparks & Mencers	31 500	units @ £3.75 = 118 125
Nat Stores	10 000	units @ £4.40 = 44 000
Smallwoods	5 000	units @ £4.00 = 20 000
Total	46 500	units TOTAL SALES £619 475

Revised sales	87.146% of £619 475	539 848
− Variable costs	87.146% of £463 163	403 628
− Overheads		110 000
= PROFIT		£26 220

Variable costs

Product A

| 61 000 | units × materials | £3.60 = 219 600 |
| | units × labour | £1.725 = 105 225 |

Product B

| 46 500 | units × materials | £2.40 = 111 600 |
| | units × labour | £0.575 = 26 738 |

| TOTAL VARIABLE COSTS | = 436 163 |

Labour hours

Product A

| 61 000 | units × 3 hr | = 183 000 |

Product B

| 46 500 | units × 1 hr | = 46 500 |

| TOTAL LABOUR HOURS | 229 500 |

Comment Labour hours available only 200 000. This represents an oversold situation. It is necessary to reduce sales and variable costs to the 200 000 hr of work the factory can handle, i.e.,

$$\frac{200\ 000}{229\ 500}\ \text{hr},$$

i.e., 87.146% of respective totals.

Fig. A.3. Profits for Group 1

Sales

Product A

Sparks & Mencers	20 000	units @ £7.85 =	157 000
Nat Stores	12 000	units @ £7.80 =	93 600
Smallwoods	20 000	units @ £7.75 =	155 000
Total	52 000	units	

Product B

Sparks & Mencers	9 000	units @ £3.75 =	33 750
Nat Stores	15 000	units @ £3.75 =	56 200
Smallwoods	20 000	units @ £3.75 =	75 000
Total	44 000	units TOTAL SALES	£570 600

− Variable costs	407 800
− Overheads	110 000
= PROFIT	52 800

Variable costs

Product A

52 000	units × materials	£3.60 =	187 200
	units × labour	£1.725 =	89 700

Product B

44 000	units × materials	£2.40 =	105 600
	units × labour	£0.575 =	25 300

TOTAL VARIABLE COSTS = 407 800

Labour hours

Product A

52 000	units × 3 hr	=	156 000

Product B

44 000	units × 1 hr	=	44 000

TOTAL LABOUR HOURS = 200 000

Comment

Fig. A.4. Profits for Group 2

Sales

Product A

Sparks & Mencers	25 000	units @ £7.67	= 191 750
Nat Stores	13 000	units @ £7.75	= 100 750
Smallwoods	10 000	units @ £7.70	= 77 000
Total	48 000	units	

Product B

Sparks & Mencers	25 000	units @ £3.90	= 97 500
Nat Stores	8 000	units @ £3.90	= 31 200
Smallwoods	8 000	units @ £3.95	= 31 600
Total	41 000	units TOTAL SALES	£529 800

– Variable costs	377 575
– Overheads	110 000
= PROFIT	42 225

Variable costs

Product A

48 000	units × materials	£3.60	= 172 800
	units × labour	£1.725	= 82 800

Product B

41 000	units × labour	£2.40	= 98 400
	units × labour	£0.575	= 23 575

TOTAL VARIABLE COSTS	= 377 575

Labour hours

Product A

48 000	units × 3 hr	= 144 000

Product B

41 000	units × 1 hr	= 41 000

TOTAL LABOUR HOURS	185 000

Comment: Undersold.

Fig. A.5. Profits for Group 3

Of the 40 teams tested:

1 team managed to make a loss of	−10 000 to Zero
3 teams made a profit between	11 000 and 20 000
6 teams made a profit between	21 000 and 30 000
9 teams made a profit between	31 000 and 40 000
8 teams made a profit between	41 000 and 50 000
6 teams made a profit between	51 000 and 60 000
4 teams made a profit between	61 000 and 70 000
2 teams made a profit between	71 000 and 80 000
1 team made a profit between	81 000 and 90 000

Glossary

Absorption costing   A method of product cost build-up where budgeted overheads are planned to be applied to (or absorbed by) the budgeted production.

Break-even   The point where total costs equal sales income and neither profit nor loss is made.

Budget   A predetermined plan expressed in financial terms, covering and coordinating all phases of a business.

Buyers' market   A market situation where supply exceeds demand, and a buyer, if he is willing to shop around, can usually get a favourable price.

Capital expenditure   The purchase of fixed assets, e.g., premises, machinery, equipment, and vehicles.

Capital-intensive industry   An industry where the production processes are substantially automated, with a high investment in plant and machinery, and where the role of operatives is largely machine minding.

Capital turnover   The number of times the capital employed in a business is turned over in a year's trading.
Formula   Sales £s ÷ Capital employed = Capital turnover.

Cash flow   The movement of funds in and out of the business, e.g., receipts from customers and payments to suppliers, employees, rating authorities, tax collectors, and so forth.

Contracting out   Making arrangements for some goods or operations to be made elsewhere, e.g., by another company or by home workers.

Contribution   That part of a product's selling price which remains after meeting the variable costs, and thereby yields a contribution to the fixed costs and profit.

Current assets   The sum of stocks (inventory), debtors and prepayments, cash, and credit balances in the bank.

Current liabilities   What is owed in the short term and technically should be liquidated in the current accounting year, e.g., creditors (suppliers), accruals, and bank overdraft.

Depreciation   An accounting convention which recognizes that, when a durable asset is purchased with an expected life beyond the current trading year, it would be incorrect to charge the entire cost against the current year's trading. The convention seeks to calculate a reasonable charge against the current year's trading, reflecting that part of the asset's life which has been consumed in the current year. For example, a machine with an estimated life of 10 years would be depreciated and charged against profits at the rate of one-tenth of its original cost in each of those 10 years.

Direct labour Labour which is performed on, can be identified with, is measureable, and is properly chargeable to, the product being made or service being performed.

Elasticity of demand The reaction of demand in response to changes in prices.

Financial liquidity The availability of cash or near cash (debtors and quickly realizable stocks) to meet the short-term demands of wages, payments to suppliers, taxes, etc.

Formula
$$\frac{\text{Cash} + \text{Debtors}}{\text{Current liabilities}} = \text{Liquid assets}$$

Fixed costs (expenses) Costs usually incurred with the provision and maintenance of facilities—premises, machinery, management, etc.—which within certain ranges of productive activity are relatively static, not moving significantly up or down in reaction to changes in the volume of production.

General operating expenses In the terminology of the retail industry, this includes administration, occupancy, and personnel department costs.

Incremental costs *See* Variable costs.

Inventory Stocks of raw materials, work-in-progress, and finished products.

Key factor That part of the production process which is not readily expandable, and through which all products must pass. The overall level of output is limited, therefore, to what this process can handle.

Labour efficiency The expression of hours earned as a percentage of hours spent.

Labour-intensive industry An industry where the production processes are not significantly automated and require a preponderant investment in people rather than plant and machinery.

Limiting factor *See* Key factor.

Margin The difference between the selling price of a product and its total cost, often expressed as a percentage of selling price. However, in the retail industry, the term is synonymous with *contribution*, i.e., the difference between selling price and the variable costs.

Mark-up The amount (usually a percentage) applied to the total product cost to arrive at a selling price.

Net worth   The value of what the company owns less what it owes. It is often the same as capital employed.

Occupancy costs   In the terminology of the retail industry, this includes: rent or N.A.V., depreciation or rental of equipment, insurance, maintenance, cleaning, heat, light and power, and other supplies and services.
Out-of-pocket costs   *See* Variable costs.
Overheads   All items of cost exclusive of those (such as materials, direct labour, etc.) which can be readily identifiable with the product being made.

Prime cost   The cost of direct materials and direct labour.
Product mix   The relative quantities of each product type which make up the whole production or sales turnover.

Retail inventory method   A method of keeping a perpetual inventory at retail selling prices, and the determination of inventory valuations based on average cost/retail price relationships. The method necessitates the maintenance of a complete running record of all changes in the money value of inventory, and all deliberate mark-ups or mark-downs.

Sellers' market   A market situation where demand exceeds supply and a seller can sometimes get a premium price.
Standard cost   An estimated cost prepared in advance of production or supply, correlating a technical specification of materials and labour to the prices and wage rates estimated for a selected period of time, with the addition of an apportionment of the overhead expenses estimated for the same period within a prescribed set of working conditions.
Standard direct labour   A technical specification of the amount of direct labour time spent on a product, evaluated at a rate of remuneration expected to obtain during a selected period of time.
Standard materials cost   A technical specification of the quantity and grade of materials to be used in the product, evaluated at the price expected to obtain during a selected period of time.
Standard minutes (hour)   Unit of Standard time, q.v.
Standard performance   The rate of output which qualified workers will naturally achieve without over-exertion as an average over the working day or shift, provided they know and adhere to the specified method and provided they are motivated to apply themselves to their work.
Standard time   The total time in which a job should be completed at standard performance, i.e., work content, contingency allowance for delay, unoccupied time, and interference allowance where applicable.
Stockturn   The frequency with which the stocks are turned over per annum.
Formula   Sales at selling price divided by the average value at selling prices of stocks held during the year (i.e., the average value at the end of each month or at the end of each quarter) = stockturn.

Subvention payment   A tax-deductible payment made by a parent company to a subsidiary company to offset the losses of the latter company. The objective is to avoid a group paying taxes on the profits of some member companies and getting no tax relief for losses of other member companies.

Transfer price   The price at which the product of one member firm/department of a group/company is transferred to an associated firm/department of the group/company.

Variable costs (expenses)   The extra costs incurred as a result of a decision to fulfil an order, and which would be avoidable if the decision had not been made. Also known as *incremental costs*, and *out-of-pocket costs*.

Working capital   Current assets less current liabilities.

INDEX

Printed by Spottiswoode Ballantyne Ltd., Colchester and London